A Scientific Assessment of the Validity of Mystical Experiences

In this book, the approach of the natural sciences is adopted to confront the ontological question of how far mystical experiences can be considered as reports of an objective reality rather than reports of subjective delusions.

Moving beyond traditional philosophical or cultural and theological interpretations of mystical phenomena, the author uses inductive inference to analyze claims made by secular and religious mystics, highlight links between altered states of consciousness and neurochemistry, and counters reductionist claims that mystical states are exclusively products of neurochemical, neurophysiological, or psychopathological factors. The text also considers the positive long-term effects of proper use of psychedelics and meditation.

This fresh approach to mystical experiences will be of interest to scholars, researchers, and postgraduate students working in the areas of psychology and neuroscience, and with an interest in mysticism in religious studies and philosophy.

Andrew C. Papanicolaou is Professor Emeritus of Clinical Neurosciences of the University of Tennessee, College of Medicine, USA, where he served as Chief of the Division of Clinical Neuroscience.

Routledge Research in Psychology

This series offers an international forum for original and innovative research being conducted across the field of psychology. Titles in the series are empirically or theoretically informed and explore a range of dynamic and timely issues and emerging topics. The series is aimed at upper-level and post-graduate students, researchers, and research students, as well as academics and scholars.

Recent titles in the series include:

Declarative Mapping Sentences in Qualitative Research
Theoretical, Linguistic, and Applied Usages
Paul M. W. Hackett

Post-Capitalist Subjectivity in Literature and Anti-Psychiatry
Reconceptualizing the Self Beyond Capitalism
Hans Skott-Myhre

A Scientific Assessment of the Validity of Mystical Experiences
Understanding Altered Psychological and Neurophysiological States
Andrew C. Papanicolaou

The Relevance of Alan Watts in Contemporary Culture
Understanding Contributions and Controversies
Edited by Peter J. Columbus

Eastern European Perspectives on Emotional Intelligence
Current developments and research
Edited by Lada Kaliská and John Pellitteri

The Psychological Basis of Moral Judgement
Philosophical and Empirical Approaches to Moral Relativism
John J. Park

For a complete list of titles in this series, please visit: https://www.routledge.com/Routledge-Research-in-Psychology/book-series/RRIP

A Scientific Assessment of the Validity of Mystical Experiences

Understanding Altered Psychological and Neurophysiological States

Andrew C. Papanicolaou

Routledge
Taylor & Francis Group
NEW YORK AND LONDON

First published 2021
by Routledge
52 Vanderbilt Avenue, New York, NY 10017

and by Routledge
2 Park Square, Milton Park, Abingdon, Oxon, OX14 4RN

Routledge is an imprint of the Taylor & Francis Group, an informa business

Library of Congress Cataloging-in-Publication Data
A catalog record for this title has been requested

ISBN: 9780367686642 (hbk)
ISBN: 9780367686659 (pbk)
ISBN: 9781003138488 (ebk)

Typeset in Bembo

by KnowledgeWorks Global Ltd.

To the memory of my brother

ἐν τῷ ὅλῳ δέ τινες αὐτὴν (τὴν ψυχὴν) μεμῖχθαί φασιν
Some say that it (the soul) pervades the universe

Aristotle

We lie in the lap of immense intelligence which makes us receivers of its truth and organs of its activity

Emerson

ἀρχὰς εἶναι τῶν ὅλων ἀτόμους καὶ κενόν, τὰ δ' ἄλλα πάντα νενομίσθαι
The principles of everything are atoms and space; all else is opinion

Democritus

Contents

About the Author

Andrew C. Papanicolaou is professor emeritus of Clinical Neurosciences, University of Tennessee, College of Medicine, where he served as chief of the Division of Clinical Neuroscience, Greece; president of the board of the Center of Applied Neuroscience, University of Cyprus and honorary member of the Hellenic Clinical Neurophysiology and Neuropsychology Societies. He has served on the board of Regents of the University of Ioannina, Greece; as director of the Center of Clinical Neuroscience in the University of Texas—Houston Medical Center and professor in the departments of neurosurgery, neurology and pediatrics of the same institution as well as adjunct professor of psychology at the University of Houston and of linguistics at Rice University. He founded and directed the Summer Institute of the International Neuropsychological Society, he founded the International Society for the Advancement of Clinical Magnetoencephalography and the post-graduate program in neuropsychology at the University of Athens. His publications include over 300 technical articles and book chapters in the areas of cerebral organization of higher functions and pre-surgical functional brain mapping, and several books ranging from clinical textbooks to theoretical and philosophical monographs.

Books by the Same Author

Papanicolaou, AC, Roberts, T, and Wheless, J (Eds) Fifty Years of Magnetoencephalography. Oxford University Press, 2020.

Papanicolaou, AC et al. Functional Brain Imaging in Cognitive Neurosciences (Greek Edition: 2019). Oxford University Press, 2017.

Papanicolaou, AC et al. Clinical Magnetoencephalography and Magnetic Source Imaging. Cambridge University Press, 2009.

Papanicolaou, AC et al. The Amnesias: A Clinical Textbook of Memory Disorders (Greek Edition: 2007). Oxford University Press, 2006.

Papanicolaou, AC Plato: Critique of the Relativists. Athens: Exandas, 2002.

Zouridakis, G, and Papanicolaou, AC A Concise Guide to Intraoperative Monitoring, CRC Press, December 2000.

Papanicolaou, AC Fundamentals of Functional Brain Imaging: A Guide to the Methods and Their Applications to Psychology and Behavioral Neurosciences. Netherlands: Swets & Zeitlinger, 1998.

Papanicolaou, AC Emotion: A Reconsideration of the Somatic Theory (Spanish edition: 2004). New York: Gordon and Breach and Harwood, 1989.

Papanicolaou, AC, and Gunter, PAY (Eds.) Bergson and Modern Thought: Towards a Unified Science. New York: Harwood Academic Publishers, 1987.

Acknowledgements

The initial impetus for writing this book was provided by my conversations over the years with my long-time friend Mr. Stan Blazyk on this topic. For this I owe him a debt of gratitude. I also wish to thank my friend and colleague, Professor Azarias Karamanlidis of the University of Thessaloniki, for reading the manuscript and correcting several oversights.

Preface

"The earliest preoccupation of man" writes the 19th century mystic and philosopher Sri Aurobindo[1] "and, as it seems, his inevitable and ultimate preoccupation,—for it survives the longest periods of skepticism and returns after every banishment,—is also the highest which his thoughts can envisage. It manifests itself in the divination of Godhead, the impulse toward perfection, the search after pure Truth and unmixed Bliss, the sense of a secret immortality. The ancient dawns of human knowledge have left us their witness to this constant aspiration; today we see a humanity satiated but not satisfied by victorious analysis of the externalities of Nature preparing to return to its primeval longings. The earliest formula of Wisdom promises to be its last,—God, Light, Freedom, Immortality." p. 1.

However, the possibility of the fulfillment of this promise is for the citizen of the 21st century, highly doubtful. There are two reasons for it. Perhaps the most fundamental of the two is that the divination of which Aurobindo writes clashes with the still dominant metaphysical[2] worldview of most scientists; a view that cannot accommodate notions like those of divinity and immortality, secret or otherwise. The second reason is the problematic nature of the mystical knowledge, which the mystic invokes.

Mystical experiences form a peculiar class of altered states of consciousness in that they feature two incompatible cardinal characteristics: first, they are said to be states of absolutely valid knowledge and, second, they are, strictly speaking, ineffable, inexpressible. They have been known for centuries as part of religious, medicinal and philosophical practices and have now become more accessible with the use of mind-altering (psychotropic) or mind revealing (psychedelic) or hallucinogenic or entheogenic[3]

1 Aurobindo, S. The Life Divine. Arya Publishing House, 1949, 139, Vol. I

2 Throughout this book, by "metaphysics" or "metaphysical" I mean statements that are beyond direct empirical verification.

3 The word "entheogen" means, "what generates God within". It was first used in 1979 by Carl A. P. Ruck; Jeremy Bigwood; Danny Staples; Jonathan Ott; R. Gordon Wasson in the article "Entheogens". Journal of Psychedelic Drugs. 1979. 11 (1–2): 145–146.

substances—the latter depending on one's presumptions and predilections. Yet, the question of their validity, although repeatedly addressed, remains unanswered. To facilitate settlement of this question, independently of theological and metaphysical preconceptions, and in strict conformity with the methods of the natural sciences, is the main aim of this inquiry.

As mentioned, the second reason the issue of the validity of the mystical experiences has not been settled is that they are ineffable. Therefore the knowledge they assert is dubious. As such it can and is interpreted in alternative and incompatible ways guided by the varying and at times warring metaphysical presumptions, theological convictions and cultural norms of the commentators who are interpreting the mystics' interpretation of the ineffable mystical fact.

It appears, however, possible to sidestep much of the difficulty if we limit our consideration to only those features of the experience that occur to mystics of all ages and cultures and recognize that the experience is characterized by two fairly distinct sets of features: Those that are attested in nearly identical form by nearly all mystics and those that are described differently in ways that demonstrably depend on each mystic's prior set of beliefs and values. The latter set of features cannot but give rise to diverse theologies or, more generally, to diverse and often incompatible metaphysical doctrines, the validity of which can never be verified. In contrast, the reliably articulated assertions about the nature of the hidden reality revealed in the mystical state constitute a secure base of fact. About these trans-subjective facts and these facts alone can the question of validity be meaningfully posed. Therefore establishing these facts is the main and most challenging task ahead.

I will therefore begin in chapter 1 of this book with a general description of the mystical experiences in order to set them apart from experiences that are not mystical although many of them are taken as such by many commentators and much of the public though rarely, if ever, by the mystics themselves. Some of the latter are beatific visions elicited by prayer, meditation and other behavioral methods of introspection and psychophysiological control; some are reliable side effects of drugs and some are clear signs of psychopathology.

In chapters 2 and 3 of this book, I comment on the various methods that mystics have employed since time immemorial across the globe and illustrate their results through extensive quotations of the mystics' own testimonies. My purpose here is to demonstrate that no matter what the method of their attainment may be, the core of the mystical state remains essentially constant. To establish that last point is especially important in cases where the experience is facilitated by the use of psychotropic drugs the study of which, after a period of prohibition, has begun to flourish once again in psychopharmacology laboratories and in clinics.

In chapter 4 of the book, the genuine or essential features of the experience are identified and distinguished from those that vary among mystics, and the dependence of the latter on the mystics' culturally-conditioned beliefs is demonstrated. The identification of these two sets of features is primarily based on the combined efforts of earlier commentators for reasons that are outlined in chapter one, below.

In chapters 5 and 6, having examined the motives and personality of the mystics and the circumstances surrounding their experiences in order to establish the degree of their dependability as witnesses, the issue of the validity of their ontological and the psychological claims is addressed. Also, given that this question of validity is not the concern of the mystics who are certain of the truth of their mystical knowledge but of those who have never attained it, the influence of prior worldviews of the latter in evaluating the relevant evidence is brought to the fore in recognition of the often veiled fact that the nature of that evidence is never the sole basis for accepting the conclusions to which it leads.

In the examination of the experiential evidence reported by the mystics I follow, as best I can, the same logic and the same procedures as those adopted routinely by scientists in examining ordinary empirical evidence. However, unlike most neuroscientists (but social scientists as well) who approach the mystical phenomena with the obvious purpose of pathologizing them, having assumed that they are expressions of some aberrant brain process, I have approached them with the quite different intention of judging whether they are veridical cognitions or delusions without having decided the issue in advance.

As for my goal, it will be achieved if I could enable the readers to satisfy their curiosity by reaching a reasonable answer to the question of validity stated above. And, if I could, to also provide those who, besides being curious, aspire to a full theoretical understanding of what the mystical state reveals, a secure base in fact on which to found their theories. Because, thus far, most theory-building has been based either on the a-critical conviction that the reports of the mystics are valid, or on the opinion that they are not, in which case, the explanations offered are either reasonable but mostly wrong, or unreasonable and worse than wrong, in that they lie well beyond the possibility of verification[4] (see chapter 5, in particular). This sort of cacophony of incompatible theories clamoring for recognition is of course, natural and unavoidable when they are developed before the facts

4 I am here referring to "explanations" of the mystical state in terms such as "persistence on inclusive, infantile ideation in the adult mind" attributed to Freud and other such statements the operational meaning of which is subject to alternative interpretations. For an extensive set of such "explanations" see Marshall, P. Mystical encounters with the natural world. New York: Oxford University Press. 2005.

to be explained by them have been firmly established[5]. Here, therefore, I mainly aspire to contribute the necessary condition that may avert such cacophonies in the future, while, at the same time avoiding the tendency, rather common in this field, of overwhelming the reader with torrents of metaphors and other dubious verbiage.

5 I consider the fact that there exist several typologies of the mystical experiences as a sure sign of disagreement regarding their nature among those who theorize about them. Moreover, the same theorists attempt to derive the correct typology mostly though arguments rather than though consideration of the phenomenology of the experiences to be found in the mystics' own testimonies. (See for example Wainwright, WJ. Mysticism. Sussex: The Harvester Press, 1981 or Hood, RW, Hill, PC and Spilka, BS. The Psychology of Religion: An empirical Approach. New York: the Guilford Press, 2018, Chapter 11). I, moreover, consider the widely divergent views regarding the nature of the experiences as the primary factor in the variation among theories. No converging theories are possible if the same data are thought of as mere by-products of brain activity (see e.g. Leuba, J H. The psychology of Religious Mysticism. New York: Harcourt, 1925) and as veridical expressions of an evolving consciousness (see e.g. de Chardin, PT. The Phenomenon of Man. New York: Harper and Row, 1959).

1 Defining Mystical States and Experiences

What Is the Mystical State and What Is Not

For several millennia, the mystical experience was the exclusive purview of the select few: the shamans, the medicine men, the religious zealots and those philosophers who desired direct knowledge of an ultimate reality hidden behind the veil of appearances. In contrast, today, with the relatively easy access to psychotropic substances nearly anyone has a chance to attain that knowledge. In addition, this fact facilitates assessment of the reliability or the repeatability of the mystical state and promotes its systematic study in laboratories and clinics. On the other hand, it lends credence to the notion that the mystical knowledge that was always considered by the mystics as absolute and absolutely certain regarding the essence of the veiled reality is nothing more than a transient and reversible change of the neurochemistry of the brain of no greater significance than any other common, drug-induced, delusion.

It is a well-known fact that these experiences have a sudden onset when they arise spontaneously or with the aid of behavioral and psychological procedures such as yoga, meditation or prayer, whereas when they are drug-induced or drug-facilitated[1], their emergence follows the rhythm specific to the particular psychotropic substance. With rare exceptions, like that of St. Gregory Palamas[2], who was said to be in the state of grace for one night and most of the next day or of the Buddha, who was said to be perpetually in that state, they are of short duration extending from few to several minutes and rarely to hours. The description of the rest of their features is based on the testimony of the mystics and on the verdict of the

1 I am calling the mystical state drug-facilitated rather than drug-induced in recognition of the fact that the substance ingested or otherwise introduced in the body is only one of the three factors that account for the mystical experience—if it occurs at all—the other two being the «set» and the «setting», that is, the personality of the individual and the circumstances or the context in which the drug is taken.

2 St. Gregory Palamas—Άγιος Γρηγόριος Παλαμάς— (1296–1357/59) Bishop of Thessaloniki and apologist of the importance and validity of the mystical experience.

commentators (some of whom were also mystics) who have studied and systematized them over the centuries.

Mystical experience is known by many other names such as "cosmic consciousness", "objective mystical experience", "illuminated vision of the world", "nature ecstasy", "unifying vision", "oceanic feeling", "natural, panenhenic"—meaning "All in One"[3], "unitive mystical state", "Satori", "Nirvana", "Kensho"—meaning "to see essence in Nature"[4], "universal consciousness", "illumination", "Uncreated Light" and many others. The names, however, provide only glimpses of some aspects of the experience or its object (or its content or referent)[5] so that to grasp its nature it is necessary to identify its defining or essential features and separate them from those that are incidental to it.

But to do so while aspiring to perfect classification accuracy would require that all reports alleging it be examined, no matter the era and the culture of their origin and the ways they were achieved. It would also require that the question regarding the similarity or identity of drug-facilitated experiences and those achieved through behavioral means be settled. This has in fact been attempted in the past in the context of the notoriouw "Good Friday" experiment, discussed in chapter 3, and in that of more recent studies all of which are discussed in chapter 3.

Moreover, the basic methods leading up to the mystical experiences will be briefly described along with reports of such experiences associated with each method. The latter cannot be but a small sample of the relevant testimonies in the same chapter selected from a vast literature for purposes of illustration only. To juxtapose the thousands of reports of all mystics in order to avoid selection bias in attempting to separate the reliable from the variable features of the mystical state is clearly impractical in that it would require several volumes and competence of a kind I do not possess. Even in that ideal case, though, the selection would have been, once again, only a small sample of the millions of never reported incidences of mystical illuminations that must have gone unreported or unregistered throughout the ages.

I, therefore, resorted to using mainly the verdicts of highly respected authorities that have summarized what they have deemed to be the essential features of the mystical experience having studied the mystics' reports,

3 From the Greek for Παν (All) and Εν (One).

4 Suzuki, DT. Zen Buddhism: Selected Writings of DT Suzuki. New York: Anchor Books, 1956, p. 103.

5 The mystical state or the mystical experience, much like any other type of experience has two aspects or it consists of two sets of features. First, features that characterize it as an event (such as time of onset, duration, intensity etc) and second, features that characterize its object or its content or referent, that is to say, what it is about. For example, a visual experience may be experience of (or knowledge of) a house; an emotional experience may the sentiment of anger, etc.

either in translations or in the original, in the literatures of different ages and cultures. Then, in chapter 5 and 6 of the book, I have juxtaposed and compared these verdicts with the results of contemporary studies in order to derive the final list of essential features the validity of which is examined in chapters 5 and 6.

Meanwhile, a preliminary and general sketch of what constitutes the mystical experience or the mystical state is necessary at this point for the purpose of orienting the readers most of whom are likely expecting tales of phantasmagoric "visions", of perceptual distortions, of extravagant imaginings, of strange synesthesias and of tempestuous emotions that are widely believed to form an essential aspect of the mystical experience. Visions, however, of any sort, are definitely not part of the mystical state because the mystics themselves do not consider them such, even though they may be temporally associated with it; usually by preceding its onset.

Parenthetically, visions are not to be confused with hallucinations. The latter appears to the person that has them as actual percepts—things that exist in the environment. Visions on the other hand are pseudo-hallucinations in that the person that has them knows that they are mental images. And, if they are considered real, as apparitions of holy personages often are, they are considered such only in the sense that they correspond to objects that exist in the spiritual world as defined by the visionary's theological convictions. Visions also differ from ordinary mental images in that they appear to the person that experiences them as if they are generated spontaneously, without his active participation, unlike the products of the conventional human faculty of imagination.

To resume, mystical experiences are not to be confused with parapsychological phenomena either. It is true that for many people "mystical" is synonymous with the "occult" in the fssollowing three senses of the word: First, in the sense of «unexplained» phenomena[6] like those of telepathy, telekinesis, clairvoyance or precognition. Second, in the sense of the practices of "mediums" and of spiritualists' mystagogies and other religious rites. Third, in the sense of the fascinating phenomena of "out of body" and "near death experiences", discussed in chapter 2, below. But the meaning of the word mystical and its cognates, at least as they will be used in this text, does not refer to any of the above. This is not to assert that mystical experiences and these phenomena are unrelated[7]. It is only to

6 Explanation of these phenomena would require radical revision of current psychophysiological and classical physical theory. See e.g. EF Kelly, A Crabtree and P Marshall (Eds) Beyond Physicalism. Lanham: Rowman and Littlefield, 2015.

7 The relation among these phenomena is argued for most comprehensively in Kelly EF, Kelly EW, Crabtree A, Gauld A, Grosso M and Greyson B. Irredussible Mind. Lanham: Rowman and Littlefield, 2007.

assert that, for the purpose of clarity, the question pursued here concerns only the former and not the latter.

Visions and phantasmagoric imaginings are common accretions to the mystical state and are commonly associated with deep emotions, often extremely disturbing ones, no matter whether the mystical state is due to drugs—the "bad trip" is a well-known phenomenon in the popular psychedelic culture—or to mortification and prayer where they have been considered daemonic influences. But, as already noted, they are definitely recognized as alien to the mystical experience[8]. It is common that they should precede the mystical experience but sometimes they are mixed with it, especially when the experience is of lesser intensity (see below).

Now, there is no scale to assess directly and quantitatively what I just called "intensity" because with the word intensity I am here alluding to a magnitude that is less quantitative and more quality-like. There are, however, approximations to accurate quantitative scales that are used for assessing drug-facilitated experiences in laboratory experiments[9]. These consist of estimates, on the part of the experimental subjects, of the "strength" or the "depth" or the «intensity» or the degree of persuasiveness of the experience relative to other, ordinary, but extremely important ones in their life. Most drug-facilitated mystical states are not authentic or fully developed ones (see chapter 3, in particular) and only a small percentage of participants in such studies report that they reach the highest level of "intensity" the scales allow.

But there is another way to separate the fully developed experiences from less developed. And that is the presence of a small cluster of features with the knowledge of the organic union of "all that exist" being the chief among them. "The ones most important, the central characteristic in which all fully developed mystical experiences agree", writes an eminent authority on mysticism, Walter Stace, "and which in the last analysis is definitive of them and serves to mark them off from other kinds of experiences, is that they involve the apprehension of an ultimate nonsensuous unity in all things, a oneness or a One to which neither the senses nor the reason can penetrate. In other words, it entirely transcends our sensory-intellectual consciousness." and, he continuous, "It should be carefully noted that only fully developed mystical experiences are necessarily apprehensive of the One. Many experiences have been recorded which lack this central feature but yet possess other mystical characteristics. These are borderline cases, which may be said to shade off from the central core of cases.

8 See e.g. Stace, WT. Mysticism and Philosophy. Los Angeles: Jeremy P. Tarcher, Inc., 1960.

9 See e.g. Barrett, FS, Bradstreet, MP, Leoutsakos, J-M S, Johnson, MW, and Griffiths RR. The Challenging Experience Questionnaire: Characterization of Challenging Experiences with Psilocybin Mushrooms. J Psychopharmacol. 2016, 30(12): 1279–1295.

They have to the central core the relation which some philosophers like to call family resemblance" pp. 14–15[10].

Few people reach that pinnacle no matter what method they may have used for its attainment. For example, in the over one thousand year history of Mount Athos, the "Holy Mountain" of the Eastern Orthodox Christianity, a recent study found testimonies of 150 mystics, only forty of whom have had experiences that would definitely qualify as genuine and fully developed ones[11]. Even allowing for the fact that many of the Eastern Orthodox mystics may have chosen not to leave testimonies—which is, in fact, the prevailing attitude among them—the number is still small considering the long history of the tradition.

Certainly, if it is indeed the case that one can attain genuine mystical experience with the aid of psychotropic substances, many more people will have the opportunity to become mystics, provided that they are willing to brave the chances of a "bad trip" the same way that those few that pursue the experience through mortification and prayer are willing to brave the "dark night of the soul" of which St. John of the Cross, a medieval Spanish mystic wrote so eloquently[12] or what in the tradition of the Eastern Orthodoxy is referred to as the "darkness of disrobement"[13].

It is a matter of debate among commentators as to whether there is only one type of fully developed, genuine experience, or two. But it appears that the oriental mystics, the medieval ones of Islam and of Western (Catholic) Christianity along with the Athonite monks are inclined to consider the type Walter Stace has called «introvertive» and in the Eastern Orthodox tradition is called "ecstatic" as the one deserving the status of the fully developed and ultimate mystical state. All agree, however, that Stace's "extrovertive" type, that in the Eastern Orthodox tradition is called contemplation "through the physical eyes"[14] also qualifies as a genuine mystical experience. Here is Stace's[15] description and differentiation of the two types: «Both are apprehensions of the One, but they reach it in different ways. The extrovertive way looks outward and through the physical senses into the external world and finds the One there. The introvertive way turns inward, introspectively, and finds the One at the bottom

10 Stace, WT. The teachings of the mystics. New York: Mentor Books, 1960.

11 Charalambidis, E Ch. The experience of Uncreated Light in the lives of Athonite saints. University of Thessaloniki, Greece, Doctoral Dissertations, 1999.

12 St. John of the Cross. Dark night of the soul. E A Peers translator from the critical edition of PS de Santa Teresa, CD. An electronic edition.

13 «γνόφος απεκδύσεως» whereby the soul sheds off all sensation, imagery and cognition. See Charalambidis E Ch. The experience of Uncreated Light in the lives of Athonite saints. University of Thessaloniki, Greece, Doctoral Dissertations, 1999.

14 «φυσικοίς οφθαλμοίς» See Charalambidis E Ch. The experience of Uncreated Light in the lives of Athonite saints. University of Thessaloniki, Greece, Doctoral Dissertations, 1999.

15 Stace, WT The teachings of the mystics. New York: Mentor Books, 1960.

of the self, at the bottom of human personality. The latter far outweighs the former in importance both in the history of mysticism and in the history of human thought generally. The introvertive way is the major strand in the history of mysticism, the extrovertive way a minor strand p. 15".

Moreover, he explains: "The extrovertive mystic with his physical senses continues to perceive the same world of trees and hills and tables and chairs as the rest of us. But he sees these objects transfigured in such a manner that the Unity shines through them....It is suggested that the extrovertive type of experience is a kind of halfway house to the introvertive. For the introvertive experience is wholly nonsensuous and nonintellectual. But the extrovertive experience is sensory-intellectual in so far as it still perceives physical objects but is nonsensuous and nonintellectual in so far as it perceives them as 'all one'" pp. 17–18.

The descriptions offered in the Eastern Orthodox tradition are essentially the same. Of the introvertive type, it is said: "The contemplation of the Uncreated Light involves before anything else the sense of living God that absorbs man entirely being an immaterial sense of the Immaterial. A spiritual sense not intellectual; a sense that seizes man with dominating power and transports him to another world but with such gentleness that he does not notice when it happens and he does not know if he is inside or outside his body. Then he knows himself so actively and deeply as never before in his ordinary life and at the same time he becomes oblivious of himself and the world.... United with this exceedingly complete sense of the living God is the awareness of light but of a light of different origin from the natural light. Then man remains within the light and becomes similar to the light he experiences and which transforms him into spirit and he cannot see and sense neither his materiality nor the materiality of the world p. 60 (translation mine)".

Moreover, of the extrovertive type it is said: "The Divine Light can be seen in all circumstances: in the darkness of night and brightness of day. The grace of God is sometimes expressed in such a manner that the perception of ones' body and of the surrounding world is retained. Then man may remain with his eyes open and see simultaneously two lights, the natural and the Divine Light. This type of seeing is called by the Holy Fathers «seeing through the natural eyes. p. 60 (translation mine)"[16].

It should be noted here that the identification of the object of mystical knowledge differs between Stace's account where it is called "One" and the Eastern Orthodox mystics' account where it is called God and Divine Light or Uncreated Light which is further interpreted by the Orthodox theologians as the Energy rather than the Essence of God. The specification of what are genuine and invariable features of the experience and

16 Archimandrite Sophrony of Essex. St. Silouan the Athonite.(Greek translation). Essex: Editions of the Holy Monastery of St. John. 8th Edition, 1999.

what are interpretations of it varying with the theological or metaphysical beliefs of the mystics will be examined in detail in chapter 4 of this book.

Comprehending the Ineffable

To have an experience—any experience—is to become cognizant or aware of something; to come to know something. This "something" the "object" of the experience or its referent, could be a sensation of pain, the percept of a house, a sentiment such as pity, an idea, or, most likely, different combinations of the above but in the case of mystical experiences, the referent could be something that you may be hard-pressed to call anything at all, except possibly "void" or "perfect nothingness". But the peculiarity of mystical knowledge does not end here: the void is at the same time something that you would also not help but call the source of everything; that which contains in it all events and things in the universe, your own self included; and which contains them not as a basket may contain apples, oranges and other objects but more like a thought that incorporates the different fleeting concepts that cohere to make it the thought that it is. And, that paradox renders the referent of the otherwise absolute and absolutely incontestable mystical knowledge ineffable; it renders it into something that cannot be described with any fidelity by the words in our vocabulary and the concepts that correspond to them.

Yet if the mystic must communicate this knowledge to those that have not been visited by it, he has no option but to communicate it using ordinary words and concepts. If he is verbally gifted—as some mystics are—he will choose those familiar concepts and words that best approximate the nature of the various aspects or features of the object, having first discerned those features in the undifferentiated unity of that very object which is at the same time the absolute void and All-That-Exists, the first principle of everything, the absolute "One".

Now to engage in the identification of each of those features that comprise the undifferentiated unity of the mystical object, the One, is a herculean task. To then match them to already known and familiar semantic categories that best approximate them is no less challenging. Both mental operations together tax even the most eloquent mystics and invite the danger of all sorts of distortions and misrepresentations of the original experience. Needless to say, this practice of conveying the essence of the mystical fact in words becomes exceedingly treacherous when a commentator, who is not a mystic, engages in it, especially in cases where the reports of mystics that are uneducated and inarticulate are concerned. But, if we are to achieve a modicum of understanding of the mystical state there is no alternative to engaging in it while remaining, throughout, aware of the possibility of error in representing the ineffable verbally.

In addition, anyone that handles mystical testimony ought to remain equally vigilant against the possibility of distorting it as one filters it through one's own preconceived notions. I am somewhat fortunate in this matter because starting as an agnostic on the issue, unencumbered by any particular theological or other metaphysical predilections as to what the features of the mystical object should be, I run reduced risks of mishandling the testimonies of mystics and the opinions of commentators in whose honesty and competence I am explicitly depending. But the risks are real and the knowledge that an error in specifying the essential features of the mystical object would invalidate any assessment of its significance is shadowing me as I proceed with this inquiry.

The most elementary prerequisite, then, of understanding and articulating any feature of the mystical experience, no less than of any other experience, is the referral of the discernible aspects of it to familiar cognitive categories. For example, I know something to be a table because I compare automatically and non-consciously the current percept to the pre-existing (in my mind) concept "table". I do the same with the sensation of red or with the sound of the wind. I recognize in the prosody of the other's voice that he is feeling pleasure or surprise or panic because I automatically refer the auditory percepts to the appropriate categories of feeling that are already established in my mind. Similarly, I understand the meaning of the symbol for the square root because I already have in mind the concept "square root". This being the case, the enormity of the problem of identifying features of the mystical experience in the absence of such categories is intimidating. Yet without finding a reasonable solution for it, any talk of assessing the validity of the experience would be superfluous.

Next, understanding anything at all, whether ordinary or mystical, varies in richness and depth depending on the number and variety of associations—mental images or response tendencies it automatically evokes. The understanding of a red light while driving, for instance, is most often confined to the tendency to step on the brakes. Rarely does one think of its brilliance and its kinship—however tenuous—to a spring rose. Sometimes, though, our ordinary understanding of things external or internal expands to include all sorts of associations that are of no practical importance and may even impede our acting efficiency. Yet it is those understandings, thus enriched with many relevant but practically superfluous associations that appear to supply deeper significance in our life and evoke affective states in us that make that life worth living. I believe that it is these latter forms of understanding that approximate, without ever reaching, the depths of significance and meaning of mystical knowledge. Therefore, for the non-mystic, it constitutes the only window that affords him glimpses of the world that the mystical knowledge reveals plainly to the mystic.

For most people, such deeper understandings are triggered by impressive natural phenomena and by the products of the fine arts. In addition, they most certainly characterize the state of "being in love" familiar to those who have been graced by it. But they are also occasioned by extremely stressful events and, for those rare scientists and philosophers who are totally immersed in the pursuit of riddles, are occasioned by "illuminations" or "epiphanies" of the solutions to these riddles. There is no point here to try to exhaust the list of the conditions that occasion such understandings and certainly no point to comment on each. To illustrate what I am trying to convey a few examples ought to suffice:

In unusually clear and moonless nights when one raises his eyes to the immensity of the visible universe, swarms of associations are likely to flood his consciousness regarding his position in that universe, his purpose, his fate as well as the reason for the existence of the very immensity that surrounds him; an immensity that asserts its presence against his previously unsuspecting mind and generates within him awe and reverence for the imposing beauty of all that exists. Some people in such circumstances may experience a sort of transport whereby from observers of the galaxy they may be rendered parts of it observing it, as it were, from the inside.

Similarly transporting are objects of art: the painting of the chair in the plain room of van Gogh, for example, and the deep sense of admiration and wonder it entails, engendered by the alchemy of the particular hues and shapes. In such a case countless unexpected associations even with the most trivial and ordinary of objects, such as a simple chair, enrich and deepen its meaning or its unsuspected significance. The same is true with the transport of music and of poetry and, definitely, with the countenance of a beloved face. The same is also true with whatever triggers those peculiar psychological states that Abraham Maslow named "peak experiences"[17].

Imagine now the number and diversity of associations that a particular perceptual object evokes to explode exponentially and to coalesce into something like the undifferentiated unity that is the mystical state. Multiply, next, the depth of your affective response to it while at the same time imagining that response to be less of a somatic and more of a mental affair, one that is not yours alone but resonates with everything around you, and you may thus achieve a partial understanding of the mystical state; a glimpse of the visage of an invisible yet luminous heavenly Aphrodite, the ineffable essence of Bliss and of Love that bestows meaning to all things loved; or gain a vague impression of the Divine Light of the mystical knowledge, more generally. But having promised not to overburden this account with verbiage that may not be, after all, nearly as informative as I have intended it to be, I will try to recapitulate, instead, what has been said thus far about the mystical experience.

17 Maslow A. Religions, Values and Peak Experiences. Columbus OH: Ohio State University Press, 1964.

The genuine mystical experience may be considered fully developed by virtue of the clear presence in it of certain key features. It is, primarily, a state of knowledge of some entity, usually "luminous" sometimes called One, which includes in some way the mystic's self, or mind, or consciousness or the mystic's "I". Experiences without clear presence in them of the key features (to be specified in chapter 4, below) may be genuine but developed to various degrees. Visions, however, apparitions and perceptual distortions along with their associated affective baggage do not qualify as mystical, as I have emphasized before. And, once again, the main purpose of describing the genuine mystical knowledge is to elucidate the question of its validity, a question extremely difficult to answer for aspects of ordinary experiences in the first place, let alone for the contents of the ineffable mystical knowledge.

This is so because the truth about things can have and does have different meanings depending on the nature of those things. Many things are considered definitely true. No one is likely to take issue, for example, with the principle of identity, with the proposition that two is more than one or with the Pythagorean theorem. But do all true things have the same ontological status? Do they all exist independently of the mind that thinks them, or are some or all of them mental constructions bearing no relation to whatever occasions them that lies outside the minds that think them? And can anything be true at all if it is just a figment of people's imagination especially when these people have always been a small minority and admit freely that the referent of their knowledge eludes their own understanding?

These are the questions to be addressed in the pages that follow. But before that, the phenomenology of the mystical state and the main ways leading up to it will be sufficiently explored to facilitate the subsequent effort of articulating the features of the genuine experiences and establishing their reliability. These are, first, the uncharted way of involuntary occurrences of the mystical state, whether spontaneous or triggered by some event; second, the way of philosophy; third, the way mortification and prayer and, fourth, the way of psychotropic substances.

Deliberate seeking of the mystical state presupposes adherence to a worldview that includes the possibility of the existence of the hidden, true reality being sought by the diligent seeker. But the existence of such a reality also impresses itself indelibly in the minds of those who have involuntarily and unintentionally entered the mystical state, even if they previously adhered to a different world legend in the context of which the idea of a hidden reality is a priori inadmissible. In either case, whereas the truth of the hidden reality is incontestable for the mystic it is by no means obvious to the un-illuminated multitudes. The latter will accept or reject the mystical testimony depending, to a large extent on the worldview they have already adopted whether deliberately or tacitly. And, since recognizing one's biases may reduce their effects on the eventual evaluation of the relevant facts of the mystical knowledge, the brief description of the two main world legends, offered in the next chapter, may render the reader a more impartial judge of the significance of the relevant facts to be presented in chapters 2 and 3 of the book.

The Two World Legends

"One conclusion was forced upon my mind at that time", William James recounts, recalling his experience under nitrous oxide sedation[18], "and my impression of its truth has ever since remained unshaken. It is that our normal waking consciousness, rational consciousness as we call it, is but one special type of consciousness, whilst all about it, parted from it by the filmiest of screens, there lie potential forms of consciousness entirely different. We may go through life without suspecting their existence; but apply the requisite stimulus, and at a touch they are there in all their completeness, definite types of mentality which probably somewhere have their field of application and adaptation. No account of the universe in its totality can be final which leaves these other forms of consciousness quite disregarded. How to regard them is the question—for they are so discontinuous with ordinary consciousness. Yet they may determine attitudes though they cannot furnish formulas, and open a region though they fail to give a map. At any rate, they forbid a premature closing of our accounts with reality". p. 377.

It is debatable whether the perennial legend of a world lurking behind the flimsy screen that defines the border of ordinary consciousness is confirmed by the mystical experiences of whether the legend is but a deliberate or even inadvertent sophistical attempt to normalize and to appropriate a species of strange and rare delusion that mystical experience may possibly be. The legend nevertheless persists in different forms since the beginning of recorded history, therefore its name: *perennial*[19].

It is sometimes whispered in uncertain tones[20] but throughout the ages, it is mostly proclaimed boldly. It now counts among its adherents, as it

18 James, W. The Varieties of Religious Experience. New York: Longmans, Green, And Co, 1917.

19 Huxley, A. The Perennial Philosophy. New York: Harper, 1944.

20 When either of the two world legends becomes dominant, it typically discourages or outright suppresses any discussions, whether scientific or metaphysical, that oppose its basic tenets. The irony of the case is that those who perpetrate the suppression believe that they do it in the interest of Truth remaining oblivious to the fact that their opponents, when they come to power, claim exactly the same. Thus, ideas opposing the "perennial" legend were—in the name of Truth—banned in the middle ages and those opposing the Democritean legend today are often banned as scientifically heretical, again, in the name of Truth. (See for example the complaints of biologists and cosmologists who infer "intelligent design" from the same data that their Neo-Darwinist colleagues and the cosmologists that champion the Democritean legend infer pure chance).

always did, the better part of humanity excepting only the majority of biologists, psychologists, neuroscientists and political scientists. It posits behind our conventional world of appearances an ageless and infinite spiritual force that generated this world or it is immanent in it; a force that endows the world with purpose and meaning; a force that is awesome but on balance benevolent; alive and conscious albeit not as a human is conscious, and one that animates the visible trajectories of the planets and the galaxies and the hypothetical motions of the minutest constituents of single atoms. A force, moreover, that accounts for the exquisite order that regulates the emergence of life forms from lifeless primordial matter and for the process that leads from single cells to whole living animals in embryogenesis. A force that also accounts for the striving of humanity to adhere to a moral code and for its drive to acquire knowledge, that is, to learn to discern the order inherent in the structure and behavior of things. Finally, a force that, in some unaccountable way, *is* or creates the rational human soul.

The nature and defining properties of that hidden force are unfathomable in spite of the allegation that it is in and all around us; and its ultimate purposes are equally occult. To capture its essence, the human mind has created countless myths and hypotheses, some complementary and some stridently discordant in many of their details. Very often humanity has believed in them so absolutely and uncompromisingly as to justify the shedding of blood and the burning and torturing and persecuting the misguided adherents of heterodoxies in order to save their souls or to punish their blindness to the orthodoxy these tales represent.

But, when the pitch of fanaticism becomes unbearably shrill, it compels the human mind to wonder if there really is a point for an infinite and benevolent force to create such a miserable world if a better and truer could have been created in its stead. To which questioning, the adherents to the legend have provided answers sometimes ludicrous in doctrinaire theological treatises and at other times cogent ones as those embedded in the stories of the great tragedians and novelists and in the musings of some metaphysicians. But those, not being sufficiently convincing in their disparity, have given impetus to an altogether different legend, bold and youthful and resolute.

This second legend, first formulated in the West by Leucippus and elaborated and promulgated far and wide by Democritus, ostracized as a delusion the notion of a hidden, true, world and all its denizens. It was subsequently submerged in relative obscurity with the passing of the classical antiquity to resurface in full force at the time of the Enlightenment and beyond. It usurped the authority of its rival in furnishing the metaphysical foundations of the sciences and of most social institutions in spite of the fact that its basic metaphysical tenets were incompatible with those of many of the founders of the very same sciences, notably of Leibnitz and Newton.

It still claims exclusive compatibility with science, not because without it science is not possible but because in most people's minds it is associated with the tremendous technical advances that marked its adoption. It is the physicalist or the materialist legend of Laplace, of Marx, of Monod, of Marcuse, of Derrida, of Freud, the Neo-Darwinists and of most existentialist philosophers. Though it too has evolved different variants, its core, since its classic formulation remains immutable. For that reason, one may call it the *Democritean* world legend.

The world is one, this legend tells us, and plainly visible. It consists of matter and energy—of atoms and the void, in its earliest formulation by Leucippus and Democritus. Here and there its material constituents are said to become organized by chance into functional units that, for reasons unknown, defy the law of universal entropy. It arose some fourteen billion years ago, give or take, again for no known reason, out of absolutely nothing, spontaneously, without a cause external to it[21].

No other world exists besides it or behind it. Thus nothing exists to supply it with purpose and meaning as it has no purpose for existing and no meaning itself, save for whatever meaning and purpose may be constructed by the conscious human mind, and attributed to it. As for the human conscious mind, it is nothing like the "soul" of the rival legend. On the contrary, it is an illusion, an epiphenomenon; that is to say, something that has no causative power; something that for no known reason evolved by virtue of lucky mutations of the genes of a consciousnessless species that preceded humanity, as did the DNA molecule, as did life, as did the universe itself.

So it behooves us to use our rationality, that is, one of the alleged products of our brain (which, being part of the purposeless physical universe is by definition foreign to purpose and meaning) to invent and construct purpose and meaning as a bulwark against the cold indifference of the universe, against the thousand evils that threaten us in this life and against the existential anxiety that tortures many of us over the presumed nothingness that awaits us after its inevitable termination. To invent, that is something like the older legend, knowing full well that it is our own creation but one we must somehow adopt as the only true and certainly useful basis for our social institutions and their underlying moral code that ought to regulate our conduct.

21 Some theorists like Hawking in his "Grand Design" have claimed that the universe arises out of the laws of quantum mechanics overlooking the fact that scientific laws whether quantum mechanical or classical describe the behavior of already existing things and have no power of engendering anything whatsoever since, according to the very same theorists, they are considered products of people's minds (rather than independently existing entities) thus implying that minds predate the universe—which is the perennial worldview that such theorists reject!

Both legends, the newer and the older, are elaborate metaphysical doctrines. They cannot be proven in the manner theorems of geometry may be proven. Nor can, for that matter, any of their constituent notions be put to direct experimental test. Nevertheless, it is still feasible, I believe, for one to decide which of the two is the more reasonable in terms of logical consistency; which of the two entails fewer or less extravagant claims and, perhaps most importantly, which of the two is favored by the preponderance of empirical indications—wherever such may be found.

Is the mystical state just another delusion, another fake fabrication of a brain and a consciousness looking desperately for a home in the cold and inhospitable universe? And why wouldn't be if all experiences are epiphenomenal fabrications? Or is it instead a reminder of the presence of an actual home of ours of which some of us have grown oblivious and which we all may enter any time by simply acknowledging its existence? This is the question that a mystic as well as the believer of either the perennial or the Democritean legend would have no reason for asking knowing already the answer, but one that haunts the non-mystic who is not endorsing wholeheartedly neither legend.

2 Unintentional and Deliberate Methods of Attaining Mystical States

Religious, Cultural, and Philosophical Perspectives

Aspects of the Mystical State

All aspiring mystics who engage in meditation with the express purpose of attaining mystical knowledge are adherents of the perennial world legend. They all believe in the higher hidden reality they crave to experience. Being certain, in advance, about the nature of that reality, they do no seek confirmation of its existence in the mystical state, although they definitely obtain it once they enter that state. Instead, they seek the "unspeakable bliss" that attends the confirmation. But the point of interest here is that some features of that revealed reality differ from one mystic to the next, and they differ reliably, depending on the particular theological and metaphysical tradition to which each mystic adheres.

Within the perennial worldview, two broad classes of such traditions can be distinguished: the theistic and the non-theistic. The first recognizes a personal God, like the God of Islam, Judaism or Christianity, direct knowledge of which the mystic strives to attain. The latter do not feature a personal God with the specific characteristics recognized in the former traditions and do not always draw the distinction between God the Creator and his Creation. Some, in fact, consider the deity as inherent in the universe and they are, in that sense, pantheistic. In these traditions, I include the philosophical one exemplified by the pantheism of Plotinus and that of the Vedantic religion and its offshoots, Buddhism and Zen Buddhism[1].

Accordingly, the reality revealed to each mystic appears to conform, partly, to his a priori notions regarding the nature of that reality: some report that that reality is God, the Creator. Others claim that the reality revealed to them is the sum total of all that exists inclusive of God, that which Plotinus, one of the earliest philosopher-mystics in the West called the One (Ἑν); Meister Eckhart, arguably one of the most respected philosopher-mystics of

1 I am not including Taoism because I could not find in the literature sufficiently clear descriptions of the content of the mystical experiences emerging in its context.

Christianity, Godhead (Gottheit); Ibn Arabi, a Moslem mystic, Haqq; the Taoist mystics Tao; the Hindu ones Brahman, and the Buddhists the Void.

Furthermore, given that, for all mystics, mystical knowledge is not mere perceiving of the ultimate reality but becoming one with it, those whose theological creed considers folly if not blasphemy the notion that the human soul or consciousness can ever become one with God, claim that they do become identical but not with God Himself, or with God's essence. Instead, they become one with the divine energy that emanates from Him. This is at least how the conflict between the mystical experience and the theological doctrine is resolved in the Eastern Orthodox tradition. In the Catholic tradition the same conflict is resolved by elaborate metaphysical argument[2].

It would therefore seem that the revealed reality in the mystical state is no more than a psychological mirage, a commonplace delusion; the delusion of fulfillment of a compelling expectation. It would seem that these alternative revealed "realities" are mere psychological constructions conditioned by each mystic's cultural, religious and metaphysical beliefs. It would consequently seem that there should be at least as many different potential referents of mystical knowledge as the religious sects and ontological doctrines that have appeared in human history. More likely, perhaps, even more than that; namely, as many as the individual mystics, given that each of them may interpret idiosyncratically every single religious and philosophical notion present in his cultural environment. Now, if that were the case, this inquiry would end right here. But it is not the case because aside from those aspects of the mystical reality that differ across mystics, there are others that form a core common to all mystical states, regardless of the particular tradition the mystic may belong and, beyond that, common also to those experiences that do not occur as a result of intentional meditation but are either spontaneous, (see next section) or are facilitated by drugs (see next chapter).

It should be noted here that the peculiar notion of mystical knowledge as a union of the knowing subject with the object known creates an additional conflict, this time not with any particular theological doctrine but with common sense: As it was previously commented ordinary knowing is always mediated by concepts we already possess: we know things by referring them to their appropriate semantic categories. But it has also been said that mystical knowledge is not mediated by any concepts; that its object does not fit any semantic category and is, for this reason, ineffable; that the contemplation or the "seeing"[3] is a direct contact, in fact,

2 See e.g. Meister Eckhard's laborious efforts at reconciling his experience with that of the Roman Catholic dogma in Stace, WT. The teachings of the mystics. New York: Mentor Books, 1960.

3 The object of mystical knowledge is often called a vision or theasis (θέασις, in the terminology of the Athonite monks) although it has no relation whatsoever with literal visions.

it is the becoming one—identical—with the contemplated object[4]. But if knowledge is not mediated by any concept it cannot be knowledge of any specific thing or any feature or attribute of anything including that of the knowing subject, the object of his knowledge and their union. Why then should one believe that the object of the mystical knowledge is God or "All-that-Exists" or God's Energy, or anything else, for that matter? Does not this contradiction render any descriptions that the mystics may venture to offer of their mystical experience invalid? Or is it, nevertheless, possible to specify features of the mystical object in spite of the fact that that object may be the undifferentiated union[5] of all that is, including the knowing subject? We will return to these questions in the next section and again in chapters 4-6, below.

Each theological or metaphysical tradition, theistic or non-theistic, involves formal procedures for attaining the mystical state that are nearly identical. They all emphasize that for the meditation to bear fruit the aspiring mystic ought to lead a life dedicated to the attainment of the mystical state. In the philosophical traditions it is a life of temperance, moderation (but not abnegation); in the theistic traditions a life of humility contrition and self-effacement and in some, a life of repentance and even mortification of the spirit and of the flesh. It is no wonder, then, that most mystics have been monks leading a life that fulfills the prerequisite of attaining the mystical state through meditation.

Besides the common intention to either behold or "merge with" the "One" or God or both or the "Void", all psychological methods of attainment of this aim share the procedure of systematic and gradual elimination from the field of awareness of all sensations, percepts, mental images, concepts and thoughts. They also share the prerequisite of suppression and silencing of all demands of the bodily needs and the extinction of all traces of emotion[6]. This, the mystics try to achieve in various ways, including, in the traditions of India, the practice of yoga. All these procedures entail exclusive and focal attending—mindfulness or meditation—centering on one elementary act, percept, or sensation which, after many rhythmical repetitions, loses its meaning and significance. This could be and usually is a visual stimulus, a mandala, for instance, or a repeated sound, such as the sound of "Om" in the traditions of Asia, or a name, as in the example of the poet laureate Tennyson, mentioned previously; a repetitive monotonous activity like breathing; or a phrase like the one typically used by

4 Thus, when the object of contemplation is God the immediate contact of the knowing subject with God is called deification (θέωσις): the knowing subject becomes God or similar to God—depending on the particular theological doctrine.

5 A term coined by Stace (see Stace, WT. The Teachings of the Mystics. New York: Mentor Books, 1960 and Stace, WT. Mysticism and Philosophy. Los Angeles: Jeremy P Tarcher, Inc., 1960).

6 The «disrobement of the soul» (απέκδυσις της ψυχής) in the Athonite tradition.

Eastern Orthodox monks: "Lord Jesus Christ son of God have mercy on me"; or focusing on a point of one's body (for which practice the aspiring mystics of Mount Athos were called, contemptuously, by their detractors "naval-gazers"[7].

Rendering oneself dazed and confused by becoming absorbed in the repetition of a meaningless act and thus emptying one's mind of any content is the sort of game that many children engage in and it is by no means a guarantee (though it is often a prerequisite) for the attainment of the mystical state. And, the fact that, most often than not, it simply leads to a type of stupor, raises the reasonable suspicion that the mystical state may be no different than that: mere stupor and daze. But reasonable as this suspicion may be, it can be maintained only by those that summarily disregard the testimony of all mystics as fraudulent or as self-deceptive.

Unintended or "Spontaneous" Mystical States

We now turn to the task of laying out the pragmatic grounds on which the readers ought to base their opinion about the significance of the mystical state, hopefully apart from any received notions they may harbor from their exposure to either of the two world legends. As for the purpose of recounting in this and in the following chapter the various ways in which mystical experiences are achieved, it is simply to illustrate the remarkable fact that their core features remain unaffected by the circumstances in which they arise and the ways and means by which they are achieved. Consequently, the readers of this and the next chapter should not expect to find in them precise instructions for how to achieve the mystical state. Nor should they expect a detailed historical exposition of the development of these ways through the centuries. Instead, they should expect to gain sufficient information about them in order to appreciate that in spite of their great diversity, results, the mystical states, are essentially the same.

Occasionally, the mystical experience emerges unexpectedly, without being deliberately sought. Most often, though, it follows deliberate and arduous procedures. These can be purely mental, like philosophical meditation, or silencing of all sensory input and all cognitive activity, or prayer. At other times, they involve additional psychophysiological discipline such as control of breathing and various ways of mortifying the flesh through long vigils, abstinence, humiliation, contrition even self-infliction of physical pain, all of which entail prolonged and intense psychophysiological stress. Finally, the experience is sought through the ingestion of psychotropic substances in the context of religious or healing ceremonies and in the context of private sessions aiming to entertain, to edify or

7 «Ομφαλοσκόποι» according to the rationalist theologian Barlaam of Calabria, the opponent of St. Gregory Palamas and critic of the meditative practices of the Athonite monks.

both. Finally, and more recently, the mystical experience is pursued in the context of formal experimental and clinical settings for addressing specific research questions exploring their therapeutic efficacy as well as the neurophysiological mechanisms associated with their production.

In this section, a few examples of unexpectedly and unintentionally occurring mystical experiences will be apposed in order for their main features and their similarity to those produced intentionally to be appreciated. One may call this way of achieving mystical knowledge "uncharted" because the psychological states that form its context vary widely from affectively positive to neutral to definitely negative, and it remains unclear whether behind this diversity lurks a common factor that triggers them. But possible triggers aside, the fact remains that the experience is not intended and it is not anticipated—a fact of great relevance in assessing whether it is purely a private mental construction as some commentators allege (see chapter 4) or whether it refers to an objective reality, that is, a reality independent of the mystic's mind. Because, clearly, the former possibility would be more likely in the event that the aspiring mystic is actively seeking to experience the hidden reality that he and others around him believe in, whereas it would be rather unusual for people to "construct" the same highly specified mental state without intending to construct it.

Moreover, the likelihood that the experience does, in fact, refer to an objective reality is enhanced when a child who is unlikely to be privy to specific aspects of the mystical state, reports it in essentially the same way that the mystics of Mount Athos or the Hindu seers of a bygone era have reported it: "The major incident in my life occurred when I was at school aged 14." relates one contemporary mystic[8]: "One hot Sunday afternoon in June 1949, lying on my back on a knoll under a lime tree, aware of the scents and sounds of summer and watching the flickering sun-light through the leaves of the lime tree, my mind went a blank—I suddenly found myself surrounded, embraced, by a white light, which seemed both to come from within me and from without, a very bright light but quite unlike any ordinary physical light. I was filled with an overwhelming sense of Love, of warmth, peace and joy—a Love far, far greater than any human love could be—utterly accepting, giving, compassionate, total Love. I seemed to sense a presence, but did not see anybody. I had the feeling of being 'one' with everything, and 'knowing' all things—whatever I wanted to know, I 'knew' instantly and directly. I had the sense of this being utter Reality, the real Real, far more 'real' and vivid than the ordinary everyday 'reality' of the physical world. I do not know how long this lasted: it did not seem to be a long time in that dimension; a minute? a

8 Franklin, J (2000). 'A spiritual biography: An account of spiritual/religious experiences from a small child to the present moment'. De Numine, 28.

few seconds? I don't know. Back again in this world, lying under the lime tree, I felt thunderstruck. What was that? What did it mean?" pp 14–17.

This experience that, as will become apparent in later chapters, does qualify as a genuine one, is not unique. The number of unsuspecting children throughout the ages who may have had such an experience and never told about it or did describe it to others but nobody thought it serious enough to record it is, of course, and will remain, unknown. Some such experiences, however, did survive oblivion. The one that follows is of the English poet laureate Tennyson who described it in a letter to one of his friends[9]: "I have never had any revelations through anæsthetics, but a kind of waking trance—this for lack of a better word—I have frequently had, quite up from boyhood, when I have been all alone. This has come upon me through repeating my own name to myself silently, till all at once, as it were out of the intensity of the consciousness of individuality, individuality itself seemed to dissolve and fade away into boundless being, and this is not a confused state but the clearest, the surest of the surest, utterly beyond words—where death was an almost laughable impossibility—the loss of personality (if so it were) seeming no extinction, but the only true life. I am ashamed of my feeble description. Have I not said the state is utterly beyond words?" p. 374.

The similarities of the two accounts are obvious and do not require further comment. True, Tennyson as a child seems to have inadvertently hit upon one of the techniques for inducing the experience (the repetition of a word or phrase until it loses its meaning) that will be described later on in this chapter, but certainly he did not seek it deliberately—not, at any rate, the first time of which he writes, nor would he be reasonably expected to have known its highly specific aspects in order to construct it, consciously or unconsciously, any more or any less than the child whose tale was quoted earlier.

In both examples, the entrance to the mystical world does not appear to have been precipitated by any remarkable psychological state. But there are plenty of recorded cases where essentially the same experience does follow either a definitely stressful or a definitely relaxed state such as the one reported by J. R. Symonds, another distinguished British poet quoted by William James[10]: "Suddenly, at church, or in company, or when I was reading, and always, I think, when my muscles were at rest, I felt the approach of the mood. Irresistibly it took possession of my mind and will, lasted what seemed an eternity, and disappeared in a series of rapid sensations which resembled the awakening from anæsthetic influence. One reason why I disliked this kind of trance was that I could not describe it

9 James, W. The Varieties of Religious Experience. New York: Longmans, Green, And Co, 1917.

10 Ibid.

to myself. I cannot even now find words to render it intelligible. It consisted in a gradual but swiftly progressive obliteration of space, time, sensation, and the multitudinous factors of experience which seem to qualify what we are pleased to call our Self. In proportion as these conditions of ordinary consciousness were subtracted, the sense of an underlying or essential consciousness acquired intensity. At last nothing remained but a pure, absolute, abstract Self. The universe became without form and void of content. But Self persisted, formidable in its vivid keenness, feeling the most poignant doubt about reality, ready, as it seemed, to find existence break as breaks a bubble round about it. And what then? The apprehension of a coming dissolution, the grim conviction that this state was the last state of the conscious Self, the sense that I had followed the last thread of being to the verge of the abyss, and had arrived at demonstration of eternal Maya or illusion, stirred or seemed to stir me up again. The return to ordinary conditions of sentient existence began by my first recovering the power of touch, and then by the gradual though rapid influx of familiar impressions and diurnal interests. At last I felt myself once more a human being; and though the riddle of what is meant by life remained unsolved, I was thankful for this return from the abyss—this deliverance from so awful an initiation into the mysteries of skepticism" p. 375.

One more example will suffice for sampling the main features of the mystical state when it emerges unexpectedly out of an affectively positive psychological state. This one details the experience of Dr. Bucke, the Canadian mystic who coined for it the term "cosmic consciousness". It is contained in his book of the same title and it is written in the third person[11]: "It was in the early spring, at the beginning of his thirty-sixth year. He and two friends had spent the evening reading Wordsworth, Shelley, Keats, Browning, and especially Whitman. They parted at midnight, and he had a long drive in a hansom (it was in an English city). His mind, deeply under the influence of the ideas, images and emotions called up by the reading and talk of the evening, was calm and peaceful. He was in a state of quiet, almost passive enjoyment. All at once, without warning of any kind, he found himself wrapped around as it were by a flame-colored cloud. For an instant he thought of fire, some sudden conflagration in the great city; the next, he knew that the light was within himself. Directly afterwards came upon him a sense of exultation, of immense joyousness accompanied or immediately followed by an intellectual illumination quite impossible to describe. Into his brain streamed one momentary lightning-flash of the Brahmic Splendor which has ever since lightened his life; upon his heart fell one drop of Brahmic Bliss, leaving thenceforward for always an aftertaste of heaven. Among other things he did not come to

11 Bucke, R.M. Cosmic Consciousness: A Study in the Evolution of the Human Mind. New York: E.P. Dutton and Company, Inc. 1901.

believe, he saw and knew that the Cosmos is not dead matter but a living Presence, that the soul of man is immortal, that the universe is so built and ordered that without any peradventure all things work together for the good of each and all, that the foundation principle of the world is what we call love and that the happiness of every one is in the long run absolutely certain. He claims that he learned more within the few seconds during which the illumination lasted than in previous months or even years of study, and that he learned much that no study could ever have taught. The illumination itself continued not more than a few moments, but its effects proved ineffaceable; it was impossible for him ever to forget what he at that time saw and knew; neither did he, or could he, ever doubt the truth of what was then presented to his mind. There was no return, that night or at any other time, of the experience. He subsequently wrote a book in which he sought to embody the teaching of the illumination. Some who read it thought very highly of it, but (as was to be expected for many reasons) it had little circulation" pp. 9–10.

As mentioned earlier, out of the exact opposite psychological climate can emerge, again unexpectedly, equally genuine mystical experiences like the one to be presented below of the well-known novelist and public intellectual, Arthur Koestler, while he was in a prison in Seville during the Spanish Civil War awaiting possible execution[12]: "I was standing at the recessed window of cell No. 40 and with a piece of iron-spring that I had extracted from the wire mattress, was scratching mathematical formulae on the wall. Mathematics, in particular analytical geometry, had been the favorite hobby of my youth, neglected later on for many years. I was trying to remember how to derive the formula of the hyperbola, and was stumped; then I tried the ellipse and parabola, and to my delight succeeded. Next I went on to recall Euclid's proof that the number of primes is infinite.... Since I had become acquainted with Euclid's proof at school, it had always filled me with a deep satisfaction that was aesthetic rather than intellectual. Now, as I recalled the method and scratched the symbols on the wall, I felt the same enchantment. And then, for the first time, I suddenly understood the reason for this enchantment: the scribbled symbols on the wall represented one of the rare cases where a meaningful and comprehensive statement about the infinite is arrived at by precise and finite means. The infinite is a mystical mass shrouded in a haze; and yet it was possible to gain some knowledge of it without losing oneself in treacly ambiguities. The significance of this swept over me like a wave. The wave had originated in an articulate verbal insight; but this evaporated at once, leaving in its wake only a wordless essence, a fragrance of eternity, a quiver of the arrow in the blue. I must have stood there for some minutes, entranced, with a wordless awareness that 'this is perfect—perfect'; until I noticed some slight mental

12 Koestler A., The Invisible Writing. New York: The Macmillan Company 1954.

discomfort nagging at the back of my mind—some trivial circumstance that marred the perfection of the moment. Then I remembered the nature of that irrelevant annoyance: I was, of course, in prison and might be shot. But this was immediately answered by a feeling whose verbal translation would be: 'So what? is that all? have you got nothing more serious to worry about?'—an answer so spontaneous, fresh and amused as if the intruding annoyance had been the loss of a collar-stud. Then I was floating on my back in a river of peace, under bridges of silence. It came from nowhere and flowed nowhere. Then there was no river and no I. The I had ceased to exist. When I say "the I had ceased to exist", I refer to a concrete experience that is verbally as incommunicable as the feeling aroused by a piano concerto, yet just as real—only much more real. In fact, its primary mark is the sensation that this state is more real than any other one has experienced before—that for the first time the veil has fallen and one is in touch with "real reality", the hidden order of things, the X-ray texture of the world, normally obscured by layers of irrelevancy. What distinguishes this type of experience from the emotional entrancements of music, landscapes or love is that the former has a definitely intellectual, or rather noumenal, content. It is meaningful, though not in verbal terms. Verbal transcriptions that come nearest to it are: the unity and interlocking of everything that exists, an interdependence like that of gravitational fields or communicating vessels. The "I" ceases to exist because it has, by a kind of mental osmosis, established communication with, and been dissolved in, the universal pool. It is the process of dissolution and limitless expansion which is sensed as the 'oceanic feeling', as the draining of all tension, the absolute catharsis, the peace that passeth all understanding."

The coming-back to the lower order of reality I found to be gradual, like waking up from anaesthesia. There was the equation of the parabola scratched on the dirty wall, the iron bed and the iron table and the strip of blue Andalusian sky. But there was no unpleasant hangover as from other modes of intoxication. On the contrary, there remained a sustained and invigorating, serene and fear-dispelling after-effect that lasted for hours and days. It was as if a massive dose of vitamins had been injected into the veins. Or, to change the metaphor, I resumed my travels through my cell like an old car with its batteries freshly recharged. Whether the experience had lasted for a few minutes or an hour, I never knew. In the beginning it occurred two or even three times a week, then the intervals became longer. It could never be voluntarily induced. After my liberation it recurred at even longer intervals, perhaps once or twice in a year. But by that time the groundwork for a change of personality was completed. I shall henceforth refer to these experiences as "the hours by the window" pp. 350–353.

I will close this short section without further comment because, I believe, no comment is needed for the reader to appreciate the similarity of the descriptions of the mystical state. This similarity is especially impressive in view of the fact that the experiences described are emphatically said to be ineffable. To show the essential identity of the unexpectedly emerging experiences with those that follow deliberate and strenuous psychological effort, several examples involving the different methods of their attainment will be presented below.

The selection of these examples is not effected randomly or in accordance with any other scientific sampling technique because their apposition is not intended to establish in an objective fashion the defining features of the genuine mystical experience. Those, as I stated earlier, are determined on the basis of the combined verdicts of a number of eminent commentators who have studied extensive samples of original reports written in different languages through the centuries. The selection of the particular reports that have been presented here and others that will be presented in the immediately following sections (along with the ways the reported experiences were attained) is simply meant to illustrate the phenomenology of experiences already deemed genuine.

I am appending here a brief summary of the descriptions of the ineffable mystical states unintentionally experienced by the four mystics quoted above, to facilitate comparison with the testimonies about mystical states deliberately sought.

About the duration of the experience they had this to say: *I don't know how long it lasted; lasted what seemed an eternity; the illumination itself continued not more than a few moments.*

About the fact that the experience was one of certain knowledge yet ineffable: *Knowing all things directly; an intellectual illumination quite impossible to describe; the state is utterly beyond words; I could not describe it to myself; It is meaningful, though not in verbal terms; a sense of this being utter reality; a concrete experience that is verbally as incommunicable as the feeling aroused by a piano concerto, yet just as real—only much more real; this state is more real than any other one has experienced before.*

About the content of the mystical knowledge: *(The sense) of (being) embraced by white light—not physical light; the light came from within; wrapped around by a flame-colored cloud; feeling one with everything; nothing remained but a pure, absolute, abstract Self; the sense that I had followed the last thread of being to the verge of the abyss; all things work together for the good of each and all; the unity and interlocking of everything that exists, an interdependence like that of gravitational fields; been dissolved in the universal pool; individuality itself seemed to dissolve and fade away into boundless being; (the state) consisted in ... obliteration of space, time, sensation, and the multitudinous factors of experience; the sense of an underlying or essential consciousness; the soul of man is immortal; The I had ceased to exist; sensed a presence; saw and knew that the Cosmos is not dead matter but a living Presence.* About the type of affect engendered by the state they said: *What distinguishes this type of experience from the emotional entrancements of music, landscapes or love is that the former has a definitely intellectual, or rather noumenal, content; warmth; Peace; floating in a river of peace; as the draining of all tension, the absolute catharsis, the peace... Joy; a sense of exultation, of immense joyousness; upon his heart fell one drop of Brahmic Bliss; Filled by Love far greater than any human love; compassion; the foundation principle of the world is what we call love; death was an almost laughable impossibility; the loss of personality seeming no extinction, but the only true life; a fragrance of eternity; I was, of course, in prison and might be shot. But this was immediately answered by a feeling whose verbal translation would be: So what? is that all?*. But also: *I was thankful for this return from the abyss—this deliverance from so awful an initiation into the mysteries.*

As for the long term after-effects of the state: *its effects proved ineffaceable; it was impossible ever to forget what he at that time saw and knew; neither would or could … ever doubt the truth of what was then presented to (the) mind; there remained a sustained and invigorating, serene and fear-dispelling after-effect that lasted for hours and days.*

The Way of the Philosophers

There is practically no doubt that, for Plato, abstract Ideas or Forms[13] and other universals such as logical or mathematical concepts are real in the sense that they exist apart from the human minds that come to know them—a belief shared by many mathematicians contemporary and older. Chief among the Forms is that of the Good in all its aspects, notably in its aspect as Beauty, which, he asserted, could be known directly through a mystical vision, and not only indirectly, through the medium of dialectics, even if only by the very few true and most tenacious lovers of wisdom.

He described the philosopher's way to the attainment of that mystical knowledge in his dialogue titled "Symposium or about Eros"[14] where he clearly distinguishes conventional or mediated, from mystical or direct knowledge through the mouth of a youthful Socrates and Socrates' old guide in matters erotic, the priestess Diotima[15]. The actual symposium on which the platonic "Symposium" was modeled, was in fact held in Athens toward the end of the fifth century the to honor the poet laureate Agathon who had just won the first prize in the dramatic festival. The discussion among those attending it was, whether in fact or only for Plato's purposes, the nature of Eros viewed as the desire of making contact with beauty—the very essence or the Form Beauty.

13 An Idea (=Iδέα) is that which is shared by a collection of things of the same kind (=Eίδος) that specifies them. It is usually translated as "Form".

14 Symposium or drinking party (Συμπόσιον). A tradition of the Athenian aristocracy of the classical era providing the setting for after dinner drinking, celebrations and discussions. This particular symposium was to celebrate the poet Agathon for being awarded the first prize in tragedy. It was attended by celebrities like Aristophanes and members of the "Socratic circle" like Phaedrus and Alcibiades. The topic of the discussion was the nature of Eros, that is, the desire to pursue beauty in its different manifestations.

15 Diotima (Διοτίμα) from Mantinea. A priestess, a philosopher and mystic whose teachings about the nature of Eros and the way of attaining Beauty—Eros' objective—are recounted by Socrates as he recalls them from a long time ago, when he was an aspiring philosopher.

The first prerequisite for attaining mystical knowledge of Beauty, we hear from Socrates' mentor, Diotima, is unrelenting devotion to the desired knowledge and its pursuit. The second is the use of the proper procedure. The procedure calls for the methodical suppression of irrelevant sensations and thoughts from the fledgling philosopher's mind in order for him to have a chance—and no more than a chance—of gaining direct knowledge of the essence of Beauty. But before that, the object of the pursuit is something specified verbally in advance, in order to direct the seeker of knowledge to his ultimate target—an aspect common to all traditions involving meditation for the attainment of mystical knowledge.

The ideal Beauty, Diotima tells Sokrates, stating clearly Plato's belief in the reality of the universals "...in the first place exists forever and it is neither generated nor lost, it is not subject to increase or to diminution. Then, is not beautiful from one point of view and ugly from another; nor is it beautiful today but not tomorrow; nor beautiful compared to this but ugly compared to that; nor beautiful here but not there, as if it were for some people beautiful and for others ugly. Moreover it will not appear to one as an aspect of a beautiful face or of beautiful hands or of anything else that has to do with the body, nor as an aspect of a discourse or of knowledge of something, or as existing as an aspect of any other thing—of an animal, for instance—or of the heaven, or of the earth, or of anything else but of something that exists by itself, independent, simple and everlasting in which all the beautiful things that come into existence and perish partake, while it remains unchanged in every way without any increase or diminution 210e–211e"[16].

To attain direct knowledge of what is merely verbally described, Socrates must learn the procedure of abstraction which consists in the gradual elimination of particular instances where Beauty is manifested: first instances perceived by the senses and then those conceived by the mind, by referring them to progressively wider, or superordinate conceptual categories. The aspiring lover of this sort of knowledge, she tells him, "may start as a youth to contemplate beautiful bodies, as his instructor may guide him, and come to love one such individual and try to help him to generate beautiful thoughts. Then he should become aware of the fact that the beauty that exists in one body is akin to the beauty of another body and given that he is pursuing the beauty of bodies in general it would be great folly for him not to recognize as one and the same the beauty that characterizes all beautiful bodies. And, once he recognizes that, he will become a lover of all beautiful people...After that he will learn to consider the beauty of the mind as superior to that of bodies...next he will recognize the beauty that characterizes

16 Plato's Symposium. Loeb Classical Library number 166. Cambridge Mass: Harvard University Press. 1996. All quotations are referenced by their chapter numbers in the original text. Translation from the original mine.

the actions of people and also the laws…and after the actions he will be lead to the beauty of thoughts and he will realize the vastness of the realm of beauty….and inspired from that realization he will produce many beautiful thoughts driven by a boundless love of knowledge until he reaches the point of maturity to acquire knowledge of the one and only Beauty 210a".

At this point the art of dialectic reaches its limits. There is nothing further to abstract. The philosopher who stops here, inspired by the realization to which dialectic has brought him, may indeed produce beautiful thoughts and equally beautiful deeds[17]. Yet he will remain ignorant of Beauty itself. And, unless he achieves his goal of making direct contact with the object of his desire he will be destitute in proportion to the extent of his unrequited Eros or Love for Beauty.

Unfortunately, most philosophers will never reach the ultimate object of their desire. They are destined to remain forever stranded before the gate to the mystical world and must be satisfied with what they have achieved, that is, visions of the "lesser mysteries" of discursive thought—a fact presented in the form of doubt Diotima expresses about the prospects of young Socrates: "To these, the lesser mysteries of Eros you too Socrates may be initiated but for the initiation to the ultimate mysteries and the revelation ….I am not sure you have what it takes" pp. 209e–210e.

Most philosophers, in fact, may only attain conventional, conceptually-mediated, knowledge of particular universals, whether of abstract moral Forms or mathematical principles, and many of them declare that no such things exist: "Any idea that I form of man must be of a specific kind of man" Bishop Berkeley states emphatically, and continuous "he must be white or black or brown, straight or crooked, tall or short or middling. Try as I may, I can't get into my mind the abstract idea …. And I find it equally impossible to form an abstract idea of motion that leaves out the thing that moves and is neither swift nor slow, curved nor straight. The same holds for absolutely all abstract ideas. I freely admit that I can perform 'abstraction' in a certain sense, namely: when several parts or qualities are united in an object, I can have the thought of one of them separated from the others if it could really exist apart from them. But I deny that I can perform 'abstraction' in the standard meaning of that word, which covers two kinds of mental performance: **(1)** conceiving abstractly and in isolation a quality that couldn't exist in isolation as we are said to do with colour and motion; and **(2)** forming a general notion by abstracting from particulars in the way I have described, as we are said to do with man and animal. There is reason to think that most people are like me in this respect. The majority of people, who are simple and illiterate, never claim

17 In Greek, the meaning of the adjective for beautiful – καλός—shades into the meaning of the adjective for good – αγαθός.

to have abstract notions. Such notions are described by those who believe in them as difficult to form; it takes hard work, we are told, to make an abstract idea. So we can reasonably conclude that if there are any abstract ideas they are all in the minds of learned people"[18].

Clearly, conventional knowledge of particular abstract notions is possible through the mediation of concrete sensory imagery. But, we are told, direct knowledge of the ultimate Form, impossible for discursive thinking and the imagination, is possible after all. Diotima, again: "whoever reaches this point when he moves forward to the end of this erotic pursuit will suddenly encounter something wondrous, Beauty itself 210a".

Beauty itself, it is suggested, is not just in the minds of learned people. It and all other objects of true knowledge exist independently of particular minds. But this is something that only the mystic who has gone through the gate of the mystical world knows. The uninitiated requires some evidence that this is indeed the case, before endorsing it; before endorsing, in fact, two different things: first that the mystical "vision" is not delusion but reality and second that aspects of that reality can be discerned by the mystic in spite of the fact that that reality is ineffable and undifferentiated.

Whether Socrates or, for that matter, Plato ever gained entrance to the mystical world just by moving toward the sealed gate propelled by his Eros for knowledge, we, most likely, will never know. There are, however, intimations throughout the Platonic corpus that Plato, did go through that gate. But whether the gate yielded to his erotic passion or whether he eased it open with the aid of Kykeon[19] as many of his compatriots did in Eleusis it is a matter that will be commented on in chapter 3.

Where Plato possibly faltered, Plotinus[20] the most celebrated mystic of the Greco-Roman antiquity must have succeeded. He tells us in his "Enneads" that he entered the mystical world several times: "Many times it has happened (to me): Lifted out of the body into myself; becoming external to all other things and self-encentered; beholding a marvellous beauty; then, more than ever, assured of community with the loftiest order; enacting the noblest life, acquiring identity with the divine; stationing within It… IV, 8, 1".

18 Berkeley, GA. treatise concerning the principles of human knowledge. Indianapolis: Hackett Publishing Company. (1710/1982) paragraph 10.

19 A potion thought to contain a psychotropic substance similar to LSD that was taken by all participants in the Eleusinian Mysteries.

20 Neo-Platonist philosopher and mystic 205-270 AD. He taught in Rome. In order to study the mysticism of India and Persia Plotinus made an unsuccessful attempt to go there, following Emperor Gordian in his ill-fated military expedition. He is the author of the Enneads (from the number nine -εννέα), six books of nine tractates each. All quotes are taken from: the Six Enneads by Plotinus. Steven Mackenna, S and B.S. Page (Translators). Global Grey e-books, 2014. All quotes are referenced by the number of the ennead (I-VI), the number of the tractate and the chapter number.

His aim in traveling there was to become aware of the primordial unity of his soul, or his self with that of the ultimate source of all that is, which he named "One"[21]. That the One did exist and that the individual souls as well as everything else that comprises the world are aspects of it he had adduced from his studies of the Platonic philosophy as well as from his knowledge of far-eastern mysticism, elements of which must have been available in Alexandria where he studied under the famous, Ammonius Saccas[22]. Therefore the purpose of his attempts at mystical enlightenment was to taste the ultimate bliss that followed the definitive proof that his ontological conclusions were correct beyond doubt. And, conviction of the ultimate, unconditional and undisputable truth of the mystically apprehended object, is one of the cardinal features of all genuine mystical states.

According to Plotinus' ontology, the ultimate reality is the Monad, the "One" which is immovable, much like Aristotle's "First Cause", immutable and eternal. From it emanates Nous or "Mind at large"[23] out of which emanate, in turn, the individual souls and all else that constitutes the familiar world. The Nous, then, that manifests itself as particular individual souls and as the rest of the entities that comprise the universe, is considered by Plotinus as a mental, not as a physical entity. As for the emanations, they are not meant as effects but as manifestations of the immutable One, much like the light rays of the sun are not effects caused by the sun but manifestations of the energy of the sun. Thus the Nous and the souls are integral parts or aspects of the One—a notion that the aspiring mystic verifies by "viewing" directly that unity or by recognizing it in the context of the mystical state.

The theory is clearly pantheistic and in that it is virtually identical to the ontology expressed in the Upanishads[24]: the One or "the Good" is both Creator in its aspect as Nous and creation since all created things are aspects or emanations of Nous as the Nous is aspect or emanation of the One. The method for directly "seeing" or encountering and establishing beyond doubt the essential identity of individual selves with One is, according to Plotinus, two-fold. It involves, first, a way of life that consists in the minimization of preoccupation with physical pleasures, disengagement from them and from other worldly concerns and in the practice of virtues as taught originally by Socrates and later by the stoic philosophers—which doctrine was also taught by the visionaries of the far-east.

21 From Ev (one or monad).

22 Ammonius Saccas of Alexandria was called the "God-taught" philosopher. He was for several years the teacher of Plotinus.

23 Mind or Nous (Νους) or the Devine Though or Energy.

24 The Upanishads form a collection of Sanskrit texts that specify the theology of Hinduism. They are the best known most recent part of the Vedas and are sometime referred to as the Vendata. They were written between 1000 and 400 BC in India.

There is no special emphasis, however, on mortification and contrition that characterizes the Christian mystical traditions: "Disengagement," Plotinus tells us, "means simply that the soul withdraws to its own place. It will hold itself above all passions and affections. Necessary pleasures and all the activity of the senses it will employ only for medicament and assuagement lest its work be impeded. Pain it may combat, but, failing the cure, it will meekly bear it and ease it by refusing to assent to it. All passionate action it will check. The suppression will be complete if that be possible, but at worst the soul will never itself take fire but will keep the involuntary and uncontrolled outside its own precincts and rare and weak at that. The soul has nothing to dread, though no doubt the involuntary has some power here too. Fear therefore must cease, except so far as it is purely monitory. What desire there may be can never be for the vile; even the food and drink necessary for restoration will lie outside the soul's attention, and not less the sexual appetite. Or, if such desire there must be, it will turn upon the actual needs of the nature and be entirely under control; or if any uncontrolled motion takes place, it will reach no further than the imagination, be no more than a fleeting fancy I, 2, 5".

Moreover, the method for attaining the mystical state according to Plotinus involves meditation on the One to the exclusion of all else, the exact procedure of which is not stated in explicit detail anywhere. This, however, is not meant to imply that the aspirant simply conjures up in his mind images or thoughts of the One because the One is beyond images and thoughts and because images and thoughts are foreign to the mystical experience. These practices, we are told, would only rarely result in the emergence of the mystical state.

Below I am quoting what seems most informative about the dialectical steps toward the attainment of the mystical experience: "We come to this learning by analogies, by abstractions, by our understanding of its subsequents, of all that is derived from The Good, by the upward steps towards it. Purification has The Good for goal; so the virtues, all right ordering, ascent within the Intellectual, settlement therein, banqueting upon the divine- by these methods one becomes, to self and to all else, at once seen and seer; identical with Being and Intellectual-Principle and the entire living all, we no longer see the Supreme as an external; we are near now, the next is That and it is close at hand, radiant above the Intellectual VI, 7, 36".

Then, having described the preparatory steps for acquiring knowledge through the practice of dialectic, Plotinus now describes the next, non-dialectical step of going through the gate of the mystical world: "Here, we put aside all the learning; disciplined to this pitch, established in beauty, the quester holds knowledge still of the ground he rests on but, suddenly, swept beyond it all by the very crest of the wave of Intellect surging beneath, he is lifted and sees, never knowing how; the vision floods the eyes with light, but it is not a light showing some other object, the light is itself the vision.

No longer is there thing seen and light to show it, no longer Intellect and object of Intellection; this is the very radiance that brought both Intellect and Intellectual object into being for the later use and allowed them to occupy the quester's mind. With This he himself becomes identical, with that radiance whose Act is to engender Intellectual-Principle, not losing in that engendering but for ever unchanged, the engendered coming to be simply because that Supreme exists VI, 7, 36".

And again: " the highest has come to her (the soul), or rather has revealed its presence; she has turned away from all about her and made herself apt, beautiful to the utmost, brought into likeness with the divine by those preparings and adornings which come unbidden to those growing ready for the vision- she has seen that presence suddenly manifesting within her, for there is nothing between: here is no longer a duality but a two in one; for, so long as the presence holds, all distinction fades: it is as lover and beloved here, in a copy of that union, long to blend; the soul has now no further awareness of being in body and will give herself no foreign name, not "man," not "living being", not "being", not "all"; any observation of such things falls away; the soul has neither time nor taste for them VI, 7, 34".

Having thus attained mystical knowledge, the soul " will barter for This nothing the universe holds; not though one would make over the heavens entire to her; than This there is nothing higher, nothing of more good; above This there is no passing; all the rest, however lofty, lies on the downgoing path: she is of perfect judgment and knows that This was her quest, that nothing higher is. Here can be no deceit; where could she come upon truer than the truth? and the truth she affirms, that she is, herself; but all the affirmation is later and is silent. In this happiness she knows beyond delusion that she is happy; for this is no affirmation of an excited body but of a soul become again what she was in the time of her early joy. All that she had welcomed of old -office, power, wealth, beauty, knowledge of all she tells her scorn as she never could had she not found their better; linked to This she can fear no disaster nor even know it; let all about her fall to pieces, so she would have it that she may be wholly with This, so huge the happiness she has won…VI, 7, 34".

The testimony of the first known philosopher-mystic in the west contains clear and unambiguous description of the main features that are found in unintentionally emerging mystical states as previously described; those that are found in contemporary testimonies of people experimenting with psychotropic substances in formal research settings; as well as those found in testimonies of mystics from the ancient traditions of India to the description of which we now turn.

The Way of the East

Even one mystical experience is sufficient, Plotinus affirms, to bestow freedom from fear and happiness. It is also sufficient, the ancient author of the

Svetasvatara Upanishad[25] tells us, to address all fundamental questions that have preoccupied humanity through the ages: "what is the cause of this Universe?—Is it Brahman? Whence do we come? Why do we live? Where we, at last, find rest? Under whose command are we bound by the law of happiness and its opposite? p. 39"[26]. And, one such experience is also sufficient to falsify the answers frequently proposed by the uninitiated adherents of the Democritean worldview: laws of nature, matter, energy time and Space, and persuade the initiated of the truth of the alternative world legend, the one revealed to Plotinus: "The seers, absorbed in contemplation, saw within themselves the ultimate reality, the self-luminous being, the one God, who dwells as the self-conscious power in all creatures". p. 40[27]

The study of the Svetasvatara Upanishad suggests that the ontology of the Hindu culture is a commentary on the truth of the mystical knowledge and makes obvious the fact that it is essentially identical to that of the Neo-Platonist mystic. Much like the ontology of Plotinus it is pantheistic in outlook. *Brahman*, the equivalent of the Plotinian One is logically anterior to all creation including individual embodied souls—*Atman* is the Sanskrit term for them—which are its manifestations: "Deep within all beings he (Brahman) dwells.... He presides over time, space and all apparent causes (parenthesis mine)"[28].

Brahman, being immutable and at rest, radiates Maya, the equivalent to Plotinus' Divine Energy or Nous, which in turn radiates the rest of the worldly creatures: "At thy bidding" sings Svetasvatara to Brahman,

> "Maya,
> Thy power Divine,
> Projects this visible Universe,
> Projects name and form"

Moreover, much like the case in the Plotinian tradition, recognition of the absolute truth of this ontology through the mystical experience is reserved for those that live a virtuous life. Such a life is the first prerequisite for the attainment of mystical knowledge. The second is the practice of meditation. The form of this practice varies within the Hindu and, later, the Buddhist and the Zen traditions but its basic elements, familiar to those that practice

25 Of the several translations of this text the one preferred by Walter Stace will be used here as well. It is to be found in: «The Upanishads: Breath of the Eternal» translated by Swami Prabhavanandana and Frederic Manchester, Hollywood, California: The Vendanta Society of Southern California. New American Library (Mentor Books), 1957. Quotes from the Upanishads used here are taken from those included in Stace's book «The teachings of the mystics. New York: Mentor Books, 1960".

26 From Stace, WT. The teachings of the mystics. New York: Mentor Books, 1960.

27 Ibid.

28 Ibid.

yoga, are summarized below: "Sit upright, holding the chest, throat, and head erect. Turn the senses and the mind inward to the lotus of the heart. Meditate on Brahman with the help of the syllable OM. Cross the fearful currents of the ocean of worldliness by means of the raft of Brahman—the sacred syllable OM. With earnest effort hold the senses in check. Controlling the breath, regulate the vital activities. As a charioteer holds back his restive horses, so does a persevering aspirant hold back his mind.

Retire to a solitary place, such as a mountain cave or a sacred spot. It must be protected from the wind and rain, and it must have a smooth, clean floor, free from pebbles and dust. It must not be damp and it must be free of disturbing noises. It must be pleasing to the eye and quieting to the mind...As you practice meditation, you may see in vision forms resembling snow, crystals, smoke, fire, lightning, fireflies, the sun, the moon. These are signs that you are on your way to the revelation of Brahman" p. 42[29].

It is worth noting two points here: first that such visual imagery is common in drug-facilitated mystical experiences as we will see in the next chapter and, second, that as in the case of the philosophic and the Plotinian road to the mystical state, there is no mention here of mortification of the flesh, contrition, repentance or sorrow that figure prominently as prerequisites in the Christian mystical traditions. This fact suggests that mortification may not be necessary since the non-stressful alternative may suffice to propel the aspiring mystic through the gate of the mystical world.

"At the gates of the transcendent" writes Sri Aurobindo,"stands that mere and perfect spirit described in the Upanishads, luminous, pure, sustaining the world...., without flaw of duality (between it and the mystic) without scar of division, unique, identical, free of all appearance of relation and multiplicity, the inactive Brahman, the transcendent Silence (reminiscent of Koestler's bridges of silence). And the mind, when it passes those gates suddenly...receives a sense of unreality of the world and the sole reality of the Silence which is one of the most powerful and convincing experiences of which the human mind is capable". (parentheses mine) p. 50.

The object, then, of the experience thus attained, is a spiritual presence, a conscious, undifferentiated unity now called Brahman or, in the Mandukya Upanishad, the entity that is "beyond the senses, beyond the understanding, beyond all expression... the pure unitary consciousness, wherein awareness of the world and of multiplicity is completely obliterated...ineffable peace...the supreme...Good. One without a second.... the Self" p. 20[30]. However expressed, knowledge of this entity is associated with uniformly positive sentiments or notions: "Only by knowing

29 Ibid.
30 Ibid.

Him does one conquer death"...knowing Him, men become immortal... Through His grace a man loses his cravings, transcends grief, and realizes Him as Brahman Supreme." pp. 43-44[31].

But even before the illumination, by simply practicing meditation "the first signs of progress on the path of yoga are health, a sense of physical lightness, clearness of complexion, a beautiful voice, an agreeable odor of the person, and freedom from craving" p. 42[32],—all of which may well have been true as a result of living a life of moderation and of physical and mental exercise as against the characteristics of the multitudes living less disciplined lives especially in the conditions of India of the fifth century BC.

The Buddhist mystical experience offers the same benefits of peace, freedom from misery and evil, and the same bliss, using the same or almost the same methods for its attainment, yet without reference to Brahman, God, Self, or to any other metaphysical entity and without explicit reference to merging of the individual self with it. Unlike Hinduism that seeks knowledge of the ultimate reality in the mystical experience, Buddhism only seeks to escape the perennial pain and suffering that afflicts humanity, the attainment of peace and the state of Bliss.

In its original formulation, Buddhism does not care about verifying the essential unity of the self with all that exists or to answer the fundamental questions that preoccupy mystical Hinduism of how everything came to be or why, since it hardly adheres to any ontology. From the religion of the Upanishads Buddhism retains only the belief in the transmigration of the souls and the cycle of rebirth and from the Hindu methods for attaining the mystical state, it retains the techniques of one of the several varieties of yoga.

However, there is no place in its doctrine for the notion of the soul of Hinduism and of all dualist metaphysical systems. Soul, in its context, is not the entity that produces the stream of perceptions, sentiments and thoughts that knows and chooses the course of a person's actions and it is held responsible for them. Instead, soul is a label for the stream of experiences—a notion akin to that of Kant's transcendental ego[33]. It is this stream of consciousness rather that than an entity that survives death and re-emerges in a new body in the cycle of metempsychosis. But the cogency of these beliefs, like the cogency of any other metaphysical notions is definitely beyond the scope of the present inquiry.

31 Ibid.

32 Ibid.

33 See e.g. James, W. Does Consciousness exist? Journal of Philosophy, Psychology and Scientific Methods. 1904 (1), 18.

Siddhartha Gautama[34], the founder of the Buddhist religion, as a young adult was struck by the fact of the ubiquitous pain and suffering that characterizes the human estate and resolved to dedicate himself to the task of finding a workable way of escaping that estate to which each person is bound to endure for millennia since the expected cycle of re-births lasted enormous stretches of time. The way he chose was suggested to him in a spontaneous mystical experience of his childhood. Remembering, as an adult, the Bliss of that remote experience he set out to attain it deliberately and teach the method of its attainment to others.

He experimented first, with extreme forms of mortification of the flesh in order to ready himself for the sought after mystical state only to discover that punishing oneself physically is not the proper preparation for the inducement of the experience. Consequently, he promoted the "middle way"—the equivalent of the Socratic moderation. Later, the proper way to prepare oneself for experiencing the mystical state was codified in an eight-step procedure.

The first step entails the internalization of a set of rational beliefs and principles of action on the part of the aspiring mystic. The second involves resolution to pursue wholeheartedly the state of illumination, called nirvana. The third, fourth and fifth steps prescribe truthfulness, engagement in activities motivated by generosity and compassion rather than selfishness, and the choice of the right profession, respectively. The latter, for those who have resolved to seek nirvana, means joining the monastic order. For the rest, it means choosing an occupation that promotes and does not compromise life as occupations like that of the slave trader do. The sixth step consists in cultivating the power of the will and applying it to overcome all distractions and obstacles to the achievement of illumination. The seventh step is to train the mind to be always aware of all actions taken, however minute and inconsequential, because lack of knowledge, according to Buddha, is principally responsible for evil—a precept that also characterizes the teachings of Socrates.

Practicing these seven steps constitutes the proper preparation for achieving nirvana much like living the virtuous life is, in the context of the Plotinian way. The eighth consists in the practice of specific techniques—a particular form of yoga—for propelling oneself through the gates of the mystical world. For the Buddhist, the purpose of entering the mystical world is not, once again, to verify any particular ontology and receive answers to the primordial metaphysical mysteries but the practical one of escaping suffering and attaining peace and happiness.

In the mystical state, the state of nirvana, the Buddhist appreciates principally the emptiness, the void created by the total suppression of all

34 A nobleman of the warier caste from northern India. He lived between the sixth and fourth centuries BC.

thoughts, sensations desires and sentiments which is also the negative aspect of the undifferentiated One of the Hindu and Plotinian tradition as well as the negative aspect of the God of the theistic traditions to be presented in the next section of this chapter. The word nirvana itself means extinction or disappearance. In attaining it, one becomes enlightened or illuminated for which the Hindi word is *Buddha*. Once Siddhartha Gautama became Buddha, the "Enlightened", it is alleged that he could enter the state of grace at will or that he remained continuously in that state until his death, fifty years later, at the age of eighty.

But is the Buddhist mystical world a true void, a total emptiness, a limitless nothing? The question has obvious bearing on the central issue of the present inquiry. Because, if this were so, then the answer to the central question as to whether the mystical knowledge is knowledge of something that exists on its own right, independently of the mystic's mind is definitely negative. There are several reasons to believe, however, that this is not the case.

In the first place, the void and the darkness or silence is one of two aspects of the experience commented by mystics of all traditions. The other aspect is the light: a *Plenum*, pregnant with everything contained in the universe; the *One* or the *Source*, or the *Universal Self*. It is true that the Buddha, unlike other mystics did avoid describing what they called incomprehensible, indescribable, inconceivable and unutterable. Yet, he did assert, albeit indirectly, that the content of mystical knowledge is something and not nothing: "There is, monks, an unborn, not become, not made, uncompounded, and were it not, monks, for this unborn, not become, not made, uncompounded, no escape could be shown here for what is born, has become, is made, is compounded. But because there is, monks, an unborn, not become, not made, uncompounded, therefore an escape can be shown for what is born, has become, is made, is compounded" p.72[35]. It does not require, I believe, elaborate interpretation, to make clear that the "unborn" is the Source of the universe, the equivalent of the Plotinian One, which makes the salvation of the creatures that emerge from it, possible.

The same point is made some centuries later by one of Buddha's heirs, Nagasena responding to a request to describe nirvana: "Is there such a thing as wind?" he asks his interlocutor, and the following conversation ensued

–"Yes, revered sir"
–"Please, sir, show the wind by its color or configuration or as thin or thick or long or short"
–"But it is not possible, revered Nagasena, for the wind to be shown…."

35 Stace, WT. The teachings of the mystics. New York: Mentor Books, 1960.

–"If, sir, it is not possible for the wind to be shown, well then, there is no wind"
–"I, revered Nagasena, know that there is wind; I am convinced of it, but I am not able to show the wind"
–"Even so, sir, nirvana exists; but it is not possible to show nirvana pp. 114–115"[36].

From such passages, earlier students of the Buddhist texts have concluded that "Nirvana is not to be thought of as a mere subjective state of mind.... at which the aspirant arrives" p. 73[37] but that it stands for something "permanent, stable, imperishable, immovable, ageless, deathless, unborn, and unbecome, that is, power bliss and happiness, the secure refuge, the shelter, and the place of unassailable safety; that it is the real truth and the supreme reality; That it is the Good; The supreme goal and the one and only consummation of our life, the eternal, hidden and incomprehensible Peace" p. 115[38].

Whether nirvana stands for all that, it is something to be decided after all the relevant indications have been apposed. But it is certain that it is all that in the opinion of those that have attained it; that it is something that has an existence independent of any particular mind and that its knowledge means escape from suffering and unequaled Bliss–the latter asserted directly by the Buddha. What the state of nirvana does not seem to include, is the knowledge of the merging or the dissolving of the self into the vastness of the One or of the Unborn and the Not Made. At least there are no allusions to that effect mentioned by the commentators of the original texts.

Nearly identical mystical experiences are attained in the context of Zen, a particular version of Buddhism that flourished in China and Japan. Zen differs from Buddhism mainly in the ways of attaining illumination or *Satori*—*Wu* in Chinese, and the equivalent of nirvana. The ways include mental exertion in dealing with paradoxical statements or enigmatic questions called *Koans* the solution or comprehension of which requires radical shifts in mental orientation, and other forms of diverting attention from ordinary reality suddenly and unexpectedly, sometimes via the sensing of physical pain[39].

36 In Smith H. Cleansing the Doors of Perception: the religious significance of entheogenic plants and chemicals. Boulder CO: Sentient Publications, 2000.

37 Stace, WT. The teachings of the mystics. New York: Mentor Books, 1960.

38 Cited in Smith H. Cleansing the Doors of Perception: the religious significance of entheogenic plants and chemicals. Boulder CO: Sentient Publications, 2000: Conze E. Buddhism: its essence and development. New York, Harper and Row 1951.

39 Like sudden blows on the part of the master to the apprentice but certainly not mortification of the flesh as practiced in the theistic traditions.

If there is a difference between the satori and other forms of mystical experience, it is not in terms of content but in that it has an abrupt onset and very brief duration. These contents are summarized by professor Suzuki, the recognized authority who brought Zen Buddhism in the West, thus: "It is noteworthy that the knowledge contained in satori is concerned with something universal and at the same time with the individual aspect of existence.... The knowledge realized in satori is final... no amount of logical argument can refute it. Being direct and personal it is sufficient unto itself. All that logic can do here is to explain it, to interpret it in connection with other kinds of knowledge with which our minds are filled. ...Though the satori experience is sometime expressed in negative terms, it is essentially an affirmative attitude towards all things that exist". And, of special significance for the present inquiry: "...in satori there is always what we may call a sense of the Beyond; The experience indeed is my own but I feel it to be rooted elsewhere. The individual shell in which my personality is so solidly encased explodes at the moment of satori. Not necessarily that I get unified with a being greater than myself or absorbed in it, but that my individuality, which I found rigidly held together and definitely kept separate from other individual existences, becomes loosened somehow from its tightening grip and melts away into something indescribable...." And again, "As far as the psychology of satori is considered, a sense of the Beyond is all we can say about it; To call this beyond the Absolute, or God or a Person is to go further than the experience itself and to plunge into a theology or metaphysics". pp. 92–93[40].

With this description, we have rounded out the main methods of preparation and meditation for the inducement of the state of mystical knowledge in the context of the non-theistic traditions. Although the description is lacking in first-hand accounts for reasons commented earlier, enough is said to indicate that the main aspects of the experience remain constant across all ways used for its attainment.

Dionysius the Areopagite and the Athonites

The ontology of the theistic religions, of Christianity, Islam and Judaism recognizes a categorical distinction between God, the Creator and His Creation. This distinction precludes absolutely any form of identification or union of the Divine essence with that of the created human soul. It is instructive, at this point, to note the effects of this relevant fact on how the mystical experience is articulated and interpreted by the theist mystics: first, although the above mentioned theological distinction clashes with the mystical experience, they still consider that the entity they come to know in the mystical state is God the Creator but, second, in spite of this

40 Stace, WT. The teachings of the mystics. New York: Mentor Books, 1960.

doctrinal prohibition they cannot help it but confess that the experience is knowledge of their union with God. Before, however, looking into the way in which the conflict of doctrinal conviction and experiential reality is adjusted, if not resolved, a few comments on the ways of attaining the mystical state in the Christian tradition are in order.

Although the doctrinal differences between the two major divisions of Christendom, namely the Eastern Orthodox and the Roman Catholic Churches, were becoming more visible as the middle age progressed, the ways of seeking the mystical experience, and the expected content of it were essentially identical. The way of seeking it was self-effacement, meditation—much the same as that of the traditions already reviewed but with an added emphasis on mortification, both of the flesh and of the mind. As for the expected and sought after content of the experience, it was God and the unification of the soul of the mystic with his God. In the following paragraphs, I will appose representative samples of the approach to the mystical knowledge of God and its realization by mystics of both Churches starting with the Eastern one.

The mystical vein is buried deeply in the otherwise rationalist theology of the Eastern Orthodox Church. It descends directly from the pre-Christian Greek culture: the Orphic and Eleusinian mysteries (of which more in the next chapter); the mysticism of Pythagoras, of Plato and Plotinus—to mention only the most familiar institutions and philosophers. This hidden vein was made conspicuous by Dionysius the Areopagite who lived in Athens in the fifth century; it was elevated later as the most direct way of salvation among the mystics of Mount Athos, the Athonites, all through the life of the Eastern Roman or Byzantine empire—a period that corresponds to the early and late middle age of western Europe; it was reconciled with the Eastern Orthodox theology and was defended against its critics by St. Gregory Palamas, and it motivates aspiring mystics to this day.

The mystical experience known in the Orthodox East as that of the "Uncreated Light"[41] is essentially the same as those that have been descried thus far. It was clearly described by Dionysius the Areopagite, albeit aphoristically, that is, by specifying what it is not, in much the same way that it is described in the Mandukya and other Upanishads and the Buddhist texts. It differs, however, from those in that it is expressing a dualist ontology whereby the mystic, the subject that has the experience, and the entity experienced remain distinct even when the former merges into the latter. This manner of articulating the experience constitutes rather clear evidence that the Areopagite's description, unlike those of his Indian

41 The term Uncreated Light (Ἄκτιστον Φῶς) appears for the first time in the works of St. Epiphanios of Salamis (315-404). See Charalambidis E Ch. The experience of Uncreated Light in the lives of Athonite saints. University of Thessaloniki, Greece, Doctoral Dissertations, 1999.

counterparts and Plotinus, was influenced by the Christian theological dogma.

But the experience described by the Areopagite is dualist in yet another way, namely, in that it entails the sharp separation of soul and body that Plato and the Neoplatonists of the Academy were teaching—which is not surprising for two reasons. First, because Dionysius is said to have been schooled by the last teachers in that slowly fading Institution, either Proclus or Damascius[42]. Second, because the theological doctrine of Christianity is fundamentally Platonic anyway.

Dionysius articulates the core features of the experience of the Uncreated Light in a letter[43] with these paradoxical statements: "The Divine *gloom* (or *darkness*) is the unapproachable *Light* which, it is said, God inhabits. And in this *gloom*, which is invisible owing to its excessive *brightness*, and unapproachable because of the excess of its superessential[44] luminance, enters the man who is deemed worthy to know and to see God, by not seeing and not knowing…(translation and parenthesis mine)".

The Uncreated Light is also darkness or gloom that surrounds God (as opposed to emanating from His essence as Plotinus expressed the same ineffable experience). The gloom here is not St. John's of the Cross "dark night of the soul"—the state preceding the mystical experience which was mentioned previously and will also be described in the next section of this chapter. Nor is it the same as the "Void" that results from the emptying of the mind of all sensations, thoughts and desires and leaving it empty, before the onset of the mystical experience. Rather, it is the undifferentiated *One* of Plotinus in which nothing particular can be discerned and which may be metaphorically likened to blindness resulting from its excessive luminance. This must be the case since the luminous darkness is not the prelude of the mystical experience but the experience itself. This light (or the One, or God's dwelling) which is called superessential, that is, beyond the essence or, more accurately, of utterly different essence than that of all created things, is allowed, by God, to be experienced only by the few worthy aspirants. Or, differently said, the grace of God allows the worthy aspirants to "enter into it" that is to merge with what is considered God's Energy or Activity but not His Essence; His energy that emanates from His essence—exactly as the Orthodox theology dictates.

However, the virtual identity of the Areopagite's description of the core features of the experience with those described in the Upanishads and by Plotinus, is obvious. What is far from obvious is the precise meaning of

42 Jones, R.M. Studies of mystical religion. London, Macmillan, 1909.

43 The fifth Epistle to the Deacon Dorotheos. In Καρανικόλας, ΠΚ. Γνόφος Αγνωσίας. Αθήναι: Αστηρ, 1980.

44 Superessential (υπερούσιος) is an often-used predicate of things divine.

the expression "to enter into" the Uncreated Light. That is, the nature of the merging, since it cannot be like the merging of the drop of water in the ocean of the totality of existing things as described by Koestler, Plotinus and the Hindu mystics, by virtue of the opposition of this notion to the "truths" of the theological doctrine.

Also unclear is whether there is anything in the experience itself that points to the nature of the light being the energy but not the essence of God; God the Creator only but not God and His Creation combined, or only His Creation. The same questions are raised by the following quotations from Dionysius' short treatise titled "Mystical Theology" where further valiant attempts are evident to articulate the ineffable content of the mystical knowledge and the methods of attaining it or, more accurately, the methods for preparing to receive it by the grace of God—which also raises the question as to whether there is something in the experience itself that points to its being a gift of God as opposed to an attainment of the mystic: "Trinity, which exceedeth all Being, Deity, and Goodness, Thou that instructeth Christians in Thy heavenly wisdom! Guide us to that topmost height of mystic lore which exceedeth light and more than exceedeth knowledge, where the simple, absolute, and unchangeable mysteries of heavenly Truth lie hidden in the dazzling obscurity of the secret Silence, outshining all brilliance with the intensity of their darkness, and surcharging our blinded intellects with the utterly impalpable and invisible fairness of glories which exceed all beauty! Such be my prayer; and thee, dear Timothy, I counsel that, in the earnest exercise of mystic contemplation, thou leave the senses and the activities of the intellect and all things that the senses or the intellect can perceive, and all things in this world of nothingness, or in that world of being, and that, thine understanding being laid to rest, thou strain (so far as thou mayest) towards an union with Him whom neither being nor understanding can contain. For, by the unceasing and absolute renunciation of thyself and all things, thou shalt in pureness cast all things aside, and be released from all, and so shalt be led upwards to the Ray of that divine Darkness which exceedeth all existence" p. 191[45].

And again,

"Unto this Darkness which is beyond Light we pray that we may come, and may attain unto vision through the loss of sight and knowledge, and that in ceasing thus to see or to know we may learn to know that which is beyond all perception and understanding (for this emptying of our faculties is true sight and knowledge), and that we may offer Him that transcends all things the praises of a transcendent hymnody, which we shall do by denying or removing all things that are… Now

45 Rolt, CE. (translator) Dionysius the Areopagite on the Divine Names and the Mystical Theology. New York: Macmillan, 1940/1957.

we must wholly distinguish this negative method from that of positive statements. …We strip off all qualities in order that we may attain a naked knowledge of that Unknowing which in all existent things is enwrapped by all objects of knowledge, and that we may begin to see that super-essential Darkness which is hidden by all the light that is in existent things." p. 194[46]

Before proceeding with the description of the experience of other mystics of the Eastern Church, it is instructive to hear the Areopagite repeat the injunction to secrecy common among the members of the Pythagorean order, of Plotinus, of the initiated in the Eleusinian mysteries (to be described in chapter 3) and all Athonite mystics past and present: "These things thou must not disclose to any of the uninitiated, by whom I mean those who cling to the objects of human thought, and imagine there is no super-essential reality beyond, and fancy they know by human understanding Him that has made Darkness His secret place. And, if the Divine Initiation is beyond such men as these, what can be said of others yet more incapable thereof, who describe the Transcendent Cause of all things by qualities drawn from the lowest order of being, while they deny that it is in any way superior to the various ungodly delusions which they fondly invent in ignorance of this truth?" p. 192[47].

What of it? one may ask. Why is it important that the uninitiated be kept in the dark about such edifying experiences that are taken as revelations of the ultimate truth and the ultimate answer of the fundamental questions that bedevil humanity? Certainly, the fear of misinterpretation of the always inadequately described experiences is one reason. Misinterpretations may well lead to adopting the wrong lifestyle on the part of the uninitiated. Also, silence about things that can be easily misunderstood may protect the mystic from persecution for imaginary evils that his experience may engender. This is reasonable but it is based on the tacit assumption on the part of the mystic that his interpretation of his experience is correct.

Yet, is there anything in the experience that indicates that all the above-mentioned assertions regarding the nature of the mystic "merging" into the Uncreated Light, or the nature of the Light or its being the gift of divine grace rather than the attainment of the mystic, is correct? After all, there is one thing to articulate—as best one can—the experience itself and quite another to hypothesize its causes and its implications since the latter are not part of the experience itself. But this distinction between the articulation of the experience and its interpretation, already made by Stace[48]

46 Ibid.
47 Ibid.
48 See e.g. Stace, WT. The teachings of the mystics. New York: Mentor Books, 1960, p. 10.

presupposes that there is an objective criterion whereby such division may be securely effected (see chapter 4).

At this point, however, one thing of relevance to the overall purpose of this inquiry must be emphasized, namely, that in some mystical traditions if not all, reluctance to publicize the attainment of what is considered the possession of the ultimate answers to the most important riddles of existence and the attainment of ultimate bliss possible in this life, is a fact. And, that this fact may be reasonably attributed to the modesty of the mystics and their indifference to notoriety and esteem rather than to fear of misinterpretations, since the Athonites have been reluctant to speak of their experience even to their peers[49].

In spite of this reluctance, several of them are known to have flourished, especially in Mount Athos in the years following the writings of Dionysius the Areopagite. They all had set as their life's goal to enter the Uncreated Light. To achieve it, they were advised, like their Buddhist counterparts, to enter the monastic life, which would provide them with the necessary preliminary training, as novices, in the virtues of self-effacement and unquestioned obedience to their mentor. Coming into their own later, they led the life of hesychasm (sacred quietude) that is, the life of self-abnegation, humility and devotion to the pursuit of the ultimate life experience: the Uncreated Light.

The life of the hesychasts attracted suspicion not only from sectors of the Byzantine laity but of the clergy as well. As it was alluded to earlier, the pursuit of mystical knowledge was deemed heretical by an also orthodox cleric from Calabria, Fr. Barlaam, who, though Greek, was schooled in the scholastic theology of the Roman Church. It was defended vigorously, however, by St. Gregory Palamas who also reconciled the experience of merging of the mystics' soul with the Uncreated Light by emphasizing the distinction between the essence of God that is totally unapproachable and his activity or Energy into which the human soul could enter.

The typical life of the aspirant mystic was that of unremitting readiness to guard against the intrusion and interference of earthly concerns with the pursuit of the mystical state and exclusive attention to that pursuit; a life-style called neptic[50], that is, one of total sobriety. It also included practicing the virtues of celibacy, poverty, humility and prudence—practices more or less the same across most religious traditions. But in the case of the Athonites, an additional set of prescriptions sets apart their specific method of pursuing the mystical state. It is the requirement that they consider themselves sinners and ask continuously for mercy and

49 Charalambidis E Ch. The experience of Uncreated Light in the lives of Athonite saints. University of Thessaloniki, Greece, Doctoral Dissertations, 1999.

50 Neptic (νηπτική) from the ancient verb nefo (νήφω) for abstaining from wine or remaining clear-headed.

absolution of their sins, which are taken for granted in all cases without exception, with tears of repentance and a marked tendency to practice the virtues of mortification to the limits of human endurance: excesses in fasting that leads to gauntness and starvation, endless vigils, genuflections and prayers, self-debasement, meanness of dress or nakedness, uncleanliness—in short severe and unrelenting punishment of body and mind that is certain to institute chronic psychosomatic stress—utterly foreign to the classical Greek ideal of moderation or, for that matter, to the Buddhist ideal of the "middle road".

As mentioned previously, in the first section of this chapter, severe stress alone, without the intention of attaining the mystical state and union with God, appears sufficient, in certain cases, to occasion the onset of that state. Yet in view of the fact that the same state can be and is attained in the absence of stress raises questions as to its role in mystical experience. Certainly, though, it did enable several Athonites to attain their sacred goal through the centuries[51]. The person that attains the blessed state is called theoptes—one who witnesses God—and is revered as such.

Moreover, by virtue of having entered the Uncreated Light rather than simply witnessing it, the theoptes is considered as having undergone a form of deification (theosis). However, unlike the mystics of the Roman church, to be discussed next in this chapter, almost all of them refrained from writing, in the first person, descriptions of their experiences. Nevertheless, the descriptions of their biographers that often include statements of the mystics themselves leave no room for doubting the authenticity of their mystical experiences. This is born out in the following quotations from Archimandrite Sofronios' of Essex biography of one of the most recent mystics, St. Silouan (1866–1938)[52].

"In beholding the Uncreated Light the dominant sense is one of the living God that absorbs the entire person; an immaterial sense of the Immaterial; a noetic[53] sense not a rational one; a sense with authority and power to transport the person to another world but with such gentleness that he does not realize at what moment this happened to him

51 The complete list of mystics is difficult to establish for two reasons: first, because it is difficult to separate true extrovertive or "through physical eyes" experiences from the "visions" of holy personages that abound in the biographies of the saints. Second because it is also difficult to tell if all the introvertive experiences were genuine because in many cases it is unclear whether the "visions" reported are mental images or metaphorical expressions of the sought after direct knowledge of Divinity.

52 Archimandrite Sophrony of Essex. St. Silouan the Athonite. (Greek translation). Essex: Editions of the Holy Monastery of St. John. 8th Edition, 1999. (Translation of all the following quotations from the Greek translation of the Russian original are mine).

53 The adjective Noetic (cognitive) derives from Νους (mind) and referred originally to knowledge or understanding of things perceived.

and he does not know if he is inside or outside his body. But he does become aware of himself so intensely and deeply, as never before in his ordinary life and at the same time he looses himself and his surroundings overwhelmed by the sweetness and love of God. Noetically he sees the Unseen, he breaths Him in being in his entirety in Him." p. 60

And: "With this sense of the living God that is beyond logic and overwhelming unites the vision of light but of a light of different kind than the natural one. Then the man remains in that light and becomes the same as the light he beholds, he is turned into spirit by It and he does not see and he does not sense neither his own materiality nor the materiality of the world" p. 60.

Moreover, "the vision comes in an incomprehensible manner when it is not expected. It does not come from the outside but neither from the inside, but in an ineffable manner surrounds the spirit of man introducing it in the world of the Divine Light. And he cannot say if that happened in ecstasy, that is outside his body because he does not perceive his return in his body either" p. 60.

And elsewhere: "…when the Lord comes to the soul of man, when the Divine Light surrounds the man entirely when the man in his entirety dwells in God, then, somehow is freedom is forfeited; his freedom feels totally given away to God and the man no longer acts on his own but he only accepts whatever he receives as gift from God. In this state, man does not ask anything. In other words, at that time all questions and all anxious speculations cease" p. 68.

The above quotations capture succinctly the main features of the ecstatic state that render it genuine in the opinion of all commentators as it will be discussed at length in chapter 4, below. But before moving on to the exposition of the mystical experience in the world of the Roman Church it will be instructive to attend to one more point: "on the basis of the data of our church's history and our communication with many monks" writes the biographer Sophronios, "we came to the conclusion that the experience of grace of those who were deemed worthy of great visitations and visions, only after many years of trials does the experience become deeply assimilated and it takes the form of spiritual knowledge. This type of knowledge, precisely, we prefer to define as 'dogmatic consciousness'. Our knowledge of history allows us to determine that a period of fifteen years or more is necessary for the assimilation of the grace. In the life of the elder Silouan we see that thirty or more years had passed before he confessed his experience in writing with mature dogmatic consciousness" p. 66.

Whether that many years are necessary for anyone to come to an understanding of his mystical experience is an empirical question that we do not need to answer here. Two things, though, I believe, are certain: First, that "dogmatic consciousness" is the referral of the experience for interpretation to the theological dogma in which the mystic believes and the reconciliation of those aspects of the experience that conflict with dogmatic orthodoxy. Certainly "dogmatic consciousness" is not necessary for articulating the experience itself. But the criteria for distinguishing articulation of the experience itself from its ex post facto interpretation will be discussed later, in chapter 4 of this inquiry.

Second, it is also certain that neither the articulation nor the interpretation of the experience can take place while the mystical state lasts. Sophronios, again: "...rational self-examination during the divine visitation not only suppresses the intensity of the sensation of the Light but it also leads in the arrest of the vision underway. In that case, the withdrawal of the grace leaves the soul naked to fall into the abyss and nothing remains in it except some abstract notion of a life from which vitality has been withheld" p. 66.

The Mystics of Western Christianity

Although there were mystics before and after Dionysius the Areopagite in the West, the most prominent ones, in the Roman Church, such as Meister Eckhart, Jan van Ruysbroeck, St. Teresa of Avila and St. John of the Cross, flourished towards the end of the middle ages. As it will become apparent, the similarity of the experiences of these mystics and those of the Athonites is striking, in spite the different metaphors used in the excerpts from their testimonies to be quoted below.

"When a person turns from temporal things inwards", writes Meister Eckhart (1260–1328) "he becomes aware of a heavenly light. ...The human spirit can never be satisfied with what light it has but storms the firmament and scales the heavens to discover the spirit by which the heavens are driven in revolutions and by which everything on the earth grows and flourishes. Even then, the human spirit takes no rest. It presses on further into the vortex, the source in which the spirit originates. There, the spirit, in knowing, has no use for number, for numbers are of use only within time, in this defective world. No one can strike his roots into eternity without being rid of number. The human spirit must go beyond all number-ideas, must break past and away from ideas of quantity and then he will be broken into by God. As God penetrates me I penetrate God in return. God leads the human spirit into the desert, into his own unity, in which he is pure One and self-creating". p. 192–193[54].

"Number" here means multiplicity of percepts, mental images and thoughts. Suppression of these is a precondition for experiencing eternity, God, and the union with God who is conceived as a desert or a "Void" (the absence of images and thoughts) or as the One of Plotinus. Notice that

54 Meister Eckhart: a modern translation. Translated by R.B. Blakney. New York and London: Harper and Brothers, 1941.

Eckhart insists in emphasizing the merging of the soul with God for which the official church chastised him: "In this barren Godhead, activity has ceased and therefore the soul will be most perfect when it is thrown into the desert of the Godhead, where both activity and forms are no more, so that it is sunk and lost in this desert where its identity is destroyed" pp. 200–201[55].

He corrects, however, the doctrinal error of his interpretation of the union of soul and God in this way: "In this exalted state she (the soul) has lost her proper self and is flowing full-flood into the unity of the divine nature. But what, you may ask, is the fate of this lost soul, does she find herself or not? ... It seems to me that...though she sinks all sinking in the oneness of divinity she never touches bottom. Wherefore God has left her one little point from which to get back to herself ... and know herself as creature" p. 282[56].

Eckhart's near contemporary, Ruysbroeck (1293–1381) confesses the same experience but he has a different interpretation of it. He feels that the Light is the second person of the Holy Trinity, the bridegroom with whom the soul of the mystic unites: "When we have thus become seeing, we can behold in joy the eternal coming of our Bridegroom... What is this coming of our Bridegroom, which is eternal? It is the new birth and a new enlightenment without interruption; for the ground from which the Light shines forth, and which is the Light itself, is life-giving and fruitful, and therefore the manifestation of the Eternal Light is renewed without ceasing" p. 171[57].

The mystical knowledge of the Deity however is only for a select minority: "Few men can attain to this Divine seeing, because of their own incapacity and the mysteriousness of the light in which one sees. And therefore no one will thoroughly understand the meaning of it by any learning or subtle consideration of his own; for all words, and all that may be learnt and understood in a creaturely way, are foreign to, and far below, the truth which I mean. But he who is united with God, and is enlightened in this truth, he is able to understand the truth by itself. For to comprehend and to understand God above all similitudes, such as He is in Himself, is to be God with God, without intermediary, and without any otherness that can become a hindrance or an intermediary" p. 167[58].

This direct knowledge requires, according to Ruysbroeck, "three things" on the part of the mystic: "The first is that he must be perfectly ordered from without in all the virtues, and within must be unencumbered, and as

55 Ibid.

56 Pfeiffer,F Meister Eckhart, translated by C de B. Evans London: J. M. Watkins, 1924, Vol. I.

57 Jan van Ruysbroeck, The Adornment of the spiritual marriage, translated by C. A. Wynschenck Dom. London: Sons, Ltd., 1916; New York: E. P. Dutton & Co., Inc, 1916.

58 Jan Van Ruysbroeck, The Adornment of the spiritual marriage, translated by C. A. Wynschenck Dom. London: Sons, Ltd., 1916.

empty of every outward work as if he did not work at all: for if his emptiness is troubled within by some work of virtue, he has an image; and as long as this endures within him, he cannot contemplate". In other words, the aspiring mystic must lead a life of virtue and empty his mind of all percepts thoughts and desires, as is recommended in all mystical traditions.

"Secondly, he must inwardly cleave to God, with adhering intention and love, even as a burning and glowing fire which can never more be quenched. As long as he feels himself to be in this state, he is able to contemplate" p. 167[59]. That is, to meditate exclusively on the object of his aim and, "Thirdly, he must have lost himself in a Waylessness and in a Darkness, in which all contemplative men wander... In the abyss of this darkness, in which the loving spirit (of the mystic) has died to itself, there begin the manifestation of God and eternal life. For in this darkness there shines and is born an incomprehensible Light, which is the Son of God, in Whom we behold eternal life. And in this Light one becomes seeing; and this Divine Light is given to the simple sight of the spirit, where the spirit receives the brightness which is God Himself, above all gifts and every creaturely activity, in the idle emptiness in which the spirit has lost itself through fruitive love, and where it receives without means the brightness of God, and is changed without interruption into that brightness which it receives. Behold, this mysterious brightness, in which one sees everything that one can desire according to the emptiness of the spirit: this brightness is so great that the loving contemplative, in his ground wherein he rests, sees and feels nothing but an incomprehensible Light; and through that Simple Nudity which enfolds all things, he finds himself, and feels himself, to be that same Light by which he sees, and nothing else. And this is the first condition by which one becomes seeing in the Divine Light. Blessed are the eyes which are thus seeing, for they possess eternal life" p. 168[60].

Whether St. Teresa of Avila (1515–1582) sought to unite with the second person of the Holy Trinity or the first, or the Godhead and the type of union she experienced is unclear because as she herself confesses "The way in which this that we call union comes, and the nature of it, I do not know how to explain. It is described in mystical theology, but I am unable to use the proper terms, and I cannot understand what is meant by 'mind' or how this differs from 'soul' or 'spirit'. They all seem the same to me"[61].

59 Ibid.

60 Ibid.

61 The complete works of Saint Teresa. Translated and edited by E. Allison Peers from the critical edition of P. Silverio de Santa Teresa, C. D. London: Sheed & Ward, Ltd., 1946; New York: Sheed & Ward, Inc., 1946, VoL I, Chapter 18.

Nevertheless, she is certain of the knowledge of a union with a living something which she calls God. She knows that her experience is of the introvertive or the ecstatic type, because during it, perception, thinking and the will are all obliterated along with the external world. She confesses that it is an experience of unspeakable bliss all of which she describes with an epistemic innocence that minimizes metaphysically driven interpretations.

She first describes the stage of emptying the mind of all sensations, thoughts and desires thus: "While seeking God in this way, the soul becomes conscious that it is fainting almost completely away, in a kind of swoon, with an exceeding great and sweet delight. It gradually ceases to breathe and all its bodily strength begins to fail it: it cannot even move its hands without great pain; its eyes involuntarily close, or, if they remain open, they can hardly see. If a person in this state attempts to read, he is unable to spell out a single letter: it is as much as he can do to recognize one. He sees that letters are there, but, as the understanding gives him no help, he cannot read them even if he so wishes. He can hear, but he cannot understand what he hears. He can apprehend nothing with the senses, which only hinder his soul's joy and thus harm rather than help him. It is futile for him to attempt to speak: his mind cannot manage to form a single word, nor, if it could, would he have the strength to pronounce it. For in this condition all outward strength vanishes, while the strength of the soul increases so that it may the better have fruition of its bliss. The outward joy experienced is great and most clearly recognized". pp. 108–109[62].

The experience itself, which she is calling rapture, she describes in these words: "I should like, with the help of God, to be able to describe the difference between union and rapture, or elevation, or what they call flight of the spirit, or transport it is all one. I mean that these different names all refer to the same thing, which is also called ecstasy. It is much more beneficial than (the term) union: the effects it produces are far more important and it has a great many more operations, for union gives the impression of being just the same at the beginning, in the middle and at the end, and it all happens interiorly. But the ends of these raptures are of a higher degree, and the effects they produce are both interior and exterior. May the Lord explain this, as He has explained everything else, for I should certainly know nothing of it if His Majesty had not shown me the ways and manners in which it can to some extent be described… In these raptures the soul seems no longer to animate the body, and thus the natural heat of the body is felt to be very sensibly diminished: it gradually becomes colder, though conscious of the greatest sweetness and delight" p. 119[63].

62 Ibid.
63 Ibid.

I believe that the "coldness" here refers to the absence of somatic contribution to the sentiments of bliss or love. This "cold" or "cerebral" or "cognitive" species of sentiment—Koestler's noetic affect—has been reported by many mystics and it is familiar to those that have experienced ecstasy with the aid of psychotropic substances (see next chapter). Also familiar is the sense of the elimination of the will and the feeling of fear when one resists surrendering control as well as the rewards of such a surrender: "You realize.... and indeed see, that you are being carried away, you know not whither. For, though rapture brings us delight, the weakness of our nature at first makes us afraid of it, and we need to be resolute and courageous in soul.... For, happen what may, we must risk everything, and resign ourselves into the hands of God and go willingly wherever we are carried away, for we are in fact being carried away, whether we like it or not. In such straits do I find myself at such a time that very often I should be glad to resist, and I exert all my strength to do so, in particular at times when it happens in public and at many other times in private, when I am afraid that I may be suffering deception. Occasionally I have been able to make some resistance, but at the cost of great exhaustion, for I would feel as weary afterwards as though I had been fighting with a powerful giant. At other times, resistance has been impossible: my soul has been borne away, and indeed as a rule my head also, without my being able to prevent it". p. 120[64].

Besides the suspicion that the rapture may not be genuine there is another motive, she claims, for resisting the experience. It is the common tendency among mystics, commented previously, to avoid publicizing their mystical experience. "I besought the Lord earnestly not to grant me any more favours which had visible and exterior signs" she writes, "for I was exhausted by having to endure such worries and after all, I said, His Majesty could grant me that favour without its becoming known". p. 120[65]. Indeed, she relates, the Lord did not grace her with such an experience in public again.

St. Teresa's description of her ruptures resembles the drug-mediated mystical experiences to a remarkable degree. Here she describes the transition of the experience from extrovertive to ecstatic where at the peak all consciousness of the external world is obliterated: "I can testify that after a rapture my body often seemed as light as if all weight had left it: sometimes this was so noticeable that I could hardly tell when my feet were touching the ground. For, while the rapture lasts, the body often remains as if dead and unable of itself to do anything: it continues all the time as it was when the rapture came upon it– in a sitting position, for example, or with the hands open or shut. The subject rarely loses consciousness: I have sometimes lost it

64 Ibid.
65 Ibid.

altogether, but only seldom and for but a short time. As a rule the consciousness is disturbed; and though incapable of action with respect to outward things, the subject can still hear and understand, but only dimly, as though from a long way off. I do not say that he can hear and understand when the rapture is at its highest point—by 'highest point' I mean when the faculties are lost through being closely united with God. At that point, in my opinion, he will neither see, nor hear, nor perceive; but, as I said in describing the preceding prayer of union, this complete transformation of the soul in God lasts but a short time, and it is only while it lasts that none of the soul's faculties is able to perceive or know what is taking place". p. 125–126[66].

Unlike St. Teresa, St John of the Cross, (1542–1591) her spiritual guide, though her junior, is more at ease in offering his psychological observations of the mystical state, but, being definitely aware of the subtleties of theological dogma, his interpretation of the state is, as definitely, conditioned by it. For him, in contrast to the dogma of the St. Gregory Palamas, the created soul is part of God. "To understand …the nature of this union" he writes, "it must be known that God dwells or is present substantially [*per substantiam*] in every soul, even in the soul of the greatest sinner… Thus, if we here speak of the union of the soul with God, we do not have in mind this ever-present substantial union, but we do mean that union of the soul with God which is consummated in the soul's transformation in God—a union which can come about only when the soul attains to a likeness with God by virtue of love. We shall therefore call this the union of likeness, to distinguish it from the union of substance or essence. The former is supernatural, the latter natural. And the supernatural union comes about when the two wills—that of the soul and that of God—are conformed in one, so that there is nothing in the one that is repugnant to the other". p. 187[67].

This conformation will follow the suppression of sensation, imagination, deliberate planning and thinking, resulting in the "night of the soul"—which night is not only the result of emptying the contents of consciousness in preparation of the entry into the mystical world but also the fact that this world is the undifferentiated unity, the divine gloom of the Areopagite: "First of all, the soul calls this dark contemplation 'secret', because, as we have indicated above, it is that mystical theology which the theologians describe as secret or hidden wisdom, and which, according to St. Thomas [Aquinas], is communicated and infused into the soul through love (cf. Summa Theologica, 2a, 2ae, q. 45, a.2). This is being done secretly, while the natural activity of the understanding and of the other faculties is in darkness. And, inasmuch as this contemplation is not brought about by any of these faculties, but is infused by the Holy Spirit,

66 Ibid.
67 Stace WT The teachings of the mystics. New York: Mentor Books, 1960.

without the soul's knowledge or understanding, it is called secret. It is not, however, for this reason alone that this contemplation may be called secret, but also because of the effects which it produces in the soul. For this contemplation is secret or hidden not only in the darknesses and afflictions of purgation, but likewise afterwards in illumination, when this wisdom is communicated to the soul with much greater clarity. Even then, however, it is still so secret that the soul is unable to name it or to speak of it. Not only has the soul no desire to speak of it or to name it, but it is unable to find any suitable similitude by which it might describe such a sublime knowledge and such a delicate spiritual experience. For this inward wisdom is so simple, general, and spiritual that it cannot enter into the understanding in any conceptual form or sensory image, notwithstanding the fact that the soul is clearly aware that it is partaking of that wondrous and blissful wisdom" pp. 196–199[68].

It will serve no purpose in quoting St. John's descriptions of the mystical experiences further, but it would be of interest to quote his opinion that mortification, including that of the flesh is of particular merit for the attainment of the experience: "There is yet another reason why the soul has walked securely in this darkness, and this is because its way has been a way of suffering. For the road of suffering is far more secure and profitable than that of rejoicing and of action: first, because in suffering man receives added strength from God, while in action and in any kind of fruition the soul is indulging its own weaknesses and imperfections; and second, because in suffering the soul activates the virtues and thus becomes purer, wiser, and more cautious" p. 197[69].

I must confess, anticipating the next section, that I am at a loss to assign any deep significance to the definite and undeniable fact that pain and suffering does sometimes trigger the mystical experience, although it is not one of its necessary conditions. But I should also repeat here that no matter what the reason for the efficacy of suffering in engendering the mystical experience might be, it does not necessarily render it trivial, as it will become clear when their validity is examined in chapter 5.

The Curious Efficacy of Mortification

It is a well-attested fact that psychosomatic stress often facilitates the onset of mystical experiences. And, the intriguing question is, why should pain and suffering, whether mental or physical and whether is visited on a person without his seeking it or is self-inflicted, be a condition that favors the attainment of the mystical state? Why is not joy or euphoria a better

68 Ibid.
69 Ibid.

precursor of the mystical state? The question has received several explanations; of those, the following appear to be the most frequent.

First is the theological explanation. It rests on the following premises: the mystical knowledge is the knowledge of God; it is bestowed by God to those who seek it if they are worthy of it; to be worthy of it means that one has paid for his sins (real or presumed—like the "original sin") and suffering is an acceptable form of atonement currency. In other words, the explanation of the efficacy of suffering as a precondition of the mystical experience rests on its value as a means of atonement. In view of that, mortification and self-immolation is not only reasonable but also necessary in the absence of punishment visited on the sinful aspirant from the outside.

Now, mortification is a very ancient practice. In some contexts, it makes perfect psychological sense in that it diverts attention from other much greater calamities when such calamities are also being visited on the individual. In the Iliad, old Priam addresses Achilles, the murderer of his son with these words: "….my eyes have yet to close under my eyelids since my boy lost his life at your hands; instead I keep on wailing and brooding over my countless woes and groveling in the barnyard dung"[70].

Self-immolation in the form of clawing one's face or pulling at one's hair in grief, if not groveling in dung, is as common a palliative in antiquity as is in our times:

> "I am burning! I am burning", cries the heroine of a modern
> poem and popular song
> "Throw more oil on the fire.
> I am drowning, I am drowning
> Throw me in a deep sea"[71]

meaning, obviously, that the agony of burning or of drowning will distract her from the far greater agonies that assail her.

In other contexts, however, the reason for mortification is not at all obvious, unless one resorts to the theological explanation previously mentioned or this one favored by many neuroscientists today (see also chapter 5, below): physical or mental pain, whether self-inflicted or not, and much like other infirmities of the brain, such as epilepsy, trauma or infection, alter the brain's biochemistry and disrupt its ordinary output which consists of ordinary experiences. The pathologically altered brain produces extraordinary, preternatural experiences, like the delusion of mystical knowledge. This explanation, also, maybe right or wrong but we will defer discussion of its status for later (chapter 5). In any case, it certainly implies that even when there is no epilepsy or trauma or any other

70 Iliad, book 24 verses 637-640. Translation mine
71 A popular Greek song by the composer Stavros Xarhakos based on lyrics by Nikos Gatsos.

infirmity, the mystical experience is still a delusion because it has been produced by some invisible, not yet diagnosed, brain dysfunction.

But there is yet another explanation. It rests on a theory clearly less parsimonious than the previous one in that it introduces a second principle, besides the brain machinery for the production of experiences but one that does not preclude the possibility that mystical knowledge is a delusion. It is a dualist theory and one that was made popular in certain circles in the first decades of the last century by Henri Bergson[72], William James[73], and Frederic W.H. Myers[74]. It was then largely ignored by the scientific establishment but not because it was formally falsified, and for that reason it is still alive among those that insist on the condition of falsification before discarding a theory[75].

In its context, the brain is viewed as a valve or a filter through which certain products of the mind—which mind exists independently of the brain—are allowed by the brain to materialize, that is, to become conscious, that is, known. Ordinarily, the brain filters out anything that does not concern the immediate vital interest of a person. In extraordinary circumstances, on the other hand, when the biochemistry of the brain is disrupted by a number of agents, including stress, the valve widens allowing the emergence, in consciousness, of extraordinary experiences like the mystical ones. Among the most vocal adherents of this theory was Aldous Huxley whose exquisite use of language lends it an aura of plausibility. He basically argued that food deprivation, whether inadvertent or voluntary, as well as self-inflicted pain and bodily injury would occasionally cause the release of the requisite amount of stress chemicals in the bloodstream that would suppress normal brain function thereby opening the (metaphorical) valve through which the wider cosmic consciousness would replace for a time the conventional one[76].

This explanation and this theory, however plausible or improbable they may now seem, could, in fact, be either right or wrong much like the previously described ones. But there is no point here to initiate a discussion about the relative validity of these three basic theories for the simple reason that the aim of this inquiry is different, albeit subtly so. Strictly speaking, the aim, once again, is whether the experiences, independently

72 Bergson, H. Matter and Memory. (N. M. Paul & W. S. Palmer, Trans.). New York: Dover Publications. 1912

73 James W. Human Immortality: Two Supposed Objections to the Doctrine (2nd ed.). Boston & New York: Houghton, Mifflin. 1900 (Original work published 1898).

74 Myers, F W H. Human Personality and Its Survival of Bodily Death (2 vols.). London: Longmans, Green, 1903.

75 See e.g. EF Kelly, A Crabtree and P Marchal (Eds) Beyond Physicalism. Lanham: Rowman and Littlefield, 2015.

76 Huxley A. the Doors of Perception and Heaven and Hell. Harper Perennial modern Classics, 1954.

of the circumstances of their production, are valid or not; whether their contents or objects have an existence of their own, independent of the brain and/or the mind that engenders them. This discussion, however, must be postponed until the mystical state and the circumstances in which it occurs are more satisfactorily outlined.

Are "Near Death Experiences" Mystical?

Extreme physiological stress of the kind that precedes death but, sometimes, mere conviction of the imminence of death, as well, in the absence of actual physiological stress, may trigger the so-called Near Death Experiences (NDEs). The experiences are sufficiently striking and unusual with features that often resemble those of the mystical state to raise the issue of whether they should be classified as such. NEDs are infrequent yet known for millennia as the ancient references to them indicate. The earliest such reference in the western literature is to be found in the tenth book of Plato's "Republic"; the second In Plutarch's myth of Thespecius of Soli in the "Moralia". In both cases, the narrative has clear moralistic intentions and in both, the procedure of Divine Judgment and the description of hell and paradise figure more prominently than the bliss, love and peace that are the most frequent hallmarks in the narratives of the NDEs of those that have experienced them in our times.

NDEs are characterized by exceptionally lucid and distinct imagery, both visual and auditory that is considered by those that have had them, more vivid, clear and real than ordinary perceptions. This feature is the single most frequent one occurring in almost all cases. Slightly less frequent but still characteristic of NDEs is their long-lasting effect on mitigating normal death anxiety that renders most people that have undergone them fearless or unconcerned about their mortality—a personality change that features prominently in mystical states as well. Between 60 and 56 percent of the NED cases[77] are also characterized by an overwhelming feeling of love, emanating from personages that greet them after they have "separated" from their bodies and view them and their surroundings (usually hospital emergency settings) from above—a feature called "Out of Body Experience" or OBE, that occurs in between 37 and 24 percent of the cases[78]. This experience is often quite puzzling because many of the events actually happening in the environment of the "lifeless" (or about to

77 As estimated in the following two publications: van Lommel, P, van Wees, R, Meyers, V, and Elfferich, I. "Near-Death Experience in Survivors of Cardiac Arrest: A Prospective Study in the Netherlands." The Lancet. 2001. Vol. 358, Issue 9298, pp. 2039-2045, and Ring, K, and Valarino, EE. Lessons from the Light: What we can learn from the near-death experience. New York: Insight Books, 2006.

78 Ibid.

become lifeless) body are reported under conditions that would normally disallow such clear and veridical perception.

Less frequent still are the experiences of going through a dark tunnel towards a light at its end; the experience of a "being of light" that may also be the source of love and bliss, and is usually considered to be God or another divinity; visions of other beings, often interpreted as angels or as gods; visions of deceased relatives and the presence of a border to permanent after-life that the people experiencing it are not allowed to cross because are either asked or compelled to "return" to their bodies. As mentioned, not all of these features appear in all cases. The most common and compelling are summarized in the now classic description of the "typical" NDE by Raymond Moody[79]:

"A man is dying and, as he reaches the point of greatest physical distress, he hears himself pronounced dead by his doctor. He begins to hear an uncomfortable noise, a loud ringing or buzzing, and at the same time feels himself moving very rapidly through a long dark tunnel. After this, he suddenly finds himself outside of his own physical body, but still in the immediate physical environment, and he sees his own body from a distance, as though he is a spectator. He watches the resuscitation attempt from this unusual vantage point and is in a state of emotional upheaval.

After a while, he collects himself and becomes more accustomed to his odd condition. He notices that he still has a "body", but one of a very different nature and with very different powers from the physical body he has left behind. Soon other things begin to happen. Others come to meet and to help him. He glimpses the spirits of relatives and friends who have already died, and a loving, warm spirit of a kind he has never encountered before—a being of light—appears before him. This being asks him a question, nonverbally, to make him evaluate his life and helps him along by showing him a panoramic, instantaneous playback of the major events of his life. At some point he finds himself approaching some sort of barrier or border, apparently representing the limit between earthly life and the next life. Yet, he finds that he must go back to the earth, that the time for his death has not yet come. At this point he resists, for by now he is taken up with his experiences in the afterlife and does not want to return. He is overwhelmed by intense feelings of joy, love, and peace. Despite his attitude, though, he somehow reunites with his physical body and lives.

Later he tries to tell others, but he has trouble doing so. In the first place, he can find no human words adequate to describe these unearthly episodes. He also finds that others scoff, so he stops telling other people. Still, the experience affects his life profoundly, especially his views about death and its relationship to life" pp. 31–32.

79 Moody, RA. Life after life. Mokingbird Books, 1975.

Narratives of this kind, if they are true rather than lies or confabulations owing to the "unearthly" nature of the experience—and many are, in fact, true—revive, in the readers' minds, the ancient conjecture of a substantial soul, entirely independent from body and brain, whose experiences, though mirrored by electrochemical events in the brain, are not their products; a soul that has a life of its own. Whether NEDs provide evidence in support of this conjecture is not the reason for discussing them in this section. Rather, the reason is, again, to determine whether they should be classified as mystical experiences. Because, whether or not they are delusions of a distressed brain, they would certainly be relevant to the aims of this book in the event they are deemed to be mystical. For that reason but also for the fact that the question of their nature is intrinsically interesting, NEDs will be briefly considered:

Are then the NDEs delusions and hallucinations of brains battling physiological stressors, like lack of oxygen due to heart failure, or indirect stressors like the (psychological) conviction of immanent death, which somehow induces physiological stress to the brain? Or, are they instead, veridical perceptions and cognitions or either still sufficiently functioning, albeit compromised brains, or perceptions of intact souls separated from compromised brains?

A number of specific phenomena, among the several that comprise each NDE, seem to point to the latter. These are, first, reports of congenitally blind patients who claimed to have visual experiences while in the NDE state[80]. Second, reports of acquisition, during NDE, of factual information from deceased relatives and friends[81] that the patient did not know they had died and, third, reports of clinically dead[82] patients that never the less claim to have perceived both, aspects of the immediate environment as well as

80 Ring, K, Cooper, S, and Tart, C. Mindsight: Near-Death and Out-of-Body Experiences in the Blind. Palo Alto, CA: William James Center for Consciousness Studies at the Institute of Transpersonal Psychology). 1999 and Ring, K, and Valarino, E E. Lessons from the Light: What we can learn from the near-death experience. New York: Insight Books. 2006.

81 Grayson, B. "Seeing Dead People Not Known to Have Died: "Peak in Darien" Experiences." American Anthropological Association. November 21, 2010. http://onlinelibrary.wiley.com/doi/10.1111/j.1548-1409.2010.01064.x/abstract.

82 Clinical death is defined by the absence of heartbeat. Twenty to thirty seconds after this event, the resulting lack of oxygen and glucose in the brain retards its function—a fact reflected in isoelectric electroencephalogram (absence of all brain rhythms) which indicates cessation of the activity of the cortex and which, almost all neuroscientists believe, is necessary for all conscious experiences. At the same time the pupils of the person are dilated and the gag reflex (which is mediated by subcortical structures) is absent. Abolition of the gag reflex is also an effect of deep anesthesia, which allows the intubation of patients and provides evidence that a patient is unconscious therefore by definition incapable of perception and all other psychological functions.

otherworldly objects and events[83]. It is the presumably accurate perception of the environment, which can be objectively verified, that is proposed as definite evidence that the reported perceptions are veridical rather than hallucinations. However, compelling as all three types of (retrospective) reports may be, they do not constitute irrefutable evidence of the type that could be furnished by a well-controlled prospective experiment[84].

Such an experiment was in fact conducted in the context of a multicenter study[85] involving resuscitation of patients that had undergone cardiac arrest. Its most relevant feature to the present discussion was the placement of signs on cards in the environment that the patients were brought for resuscitation but on top of cabinets such that they could only be viewed from vantage points above the floor by someone floating near the ceiling of the room. Of the 2060 patients examined in that study, 9% had NDEs, 2% of those reported that they had seen and heard actual events related to their resuscitation, only one patient had a verifiable period of conscious awareness during which time cerebral function was not expected, and no one reported reading or detecting the strategically placed signs.

Although those data do not demonstrate conclusively whether NDEs include veridical perceptions or delusions, they do leave us with the nagging question as to how it can be possible that clinically dead people can have any experiences whatsoever. Epsecially so, since the experiences, whether delusions and hallucinations or veridical ones are so lucid, detailed, and unforgettable. But is the brain actually inactive during NDEs? It certainly seems so in several cases but especially in the surgical case of a patient named Pam Reynolds described by a cardiologist who verified several "perceptions" of the patient against the testimonies of the operating room personnel[86].

The patient was operated for a large and inaccessible brain aneurysm. The operation required a procedure called hypothermic cardiac arrest that involves cooling the patient's blood and draining it before repairing the aneurysm and then returning the blood to the patient's circulatory system

83 See e.g. Greyson, B. "Comments on 'Does Paranormal Perception Occur in Near-Death Experiences?'" in Journal of Near-Death Studies, 2007, 25(4). pp. 237-244 and Holden, J. Handbook of Near Death Experiences: Thirty Years of Investigation. Connecticut: Praeger Press, 2009.

84 See a thorough discussion of this issue in Kelly EW, Grayson B. and Kelly EF. Chapter 6: Unusual experiences near death and related phenomena. In Kelly EF, Kelly EW, Crabtree A, Gauld A, Grosso M and Greyson B. Irreducible Mind. Lanham: Rowman and Littlefield, 2007.

85 Parnia, S. et al. "AWARE – Awareness during Resuscitation – A Prospective Study" Journal of Resuscitation (October 6, 2014).

86 Sabom, M. Light and Death: One Doctor's Fascinating Account of Near Death Experiences. Grand Rapids MI: Zondervan, 1988.

and restarting her heart that was stopped with an injection of potassium chloride.

First, the patient was anesthetized so that she could be intubated. From that point on she was rendered unconscious until the conclusion of the operation, hours later. Following anesthesia induction, her eyes were taped shut and molded speakers were placed on both her ears for delivering trains of loud clicks for monitoring, throughout the procedure, her brainstem function by means of brainstem evoked potentials. The speakers and the clicks essentially isolated her acoustically from the environment except for the end of the procedure, during closing, when brainstem response monitoring was not necessary.

While anesthetized the patient later reported hearing the noise of the saw used to cut her skull bone, which started one and one-half hour after anesthesia induction. After that she experienced leaving her body, floating over the surgeon's shoulder and seeing her shaved head that, to her, was an unexpected sight and the particular type of saw the surgeon used, which she described accurately. She also heard from her vantage point (but did not see) a female commenting on the size of her blood vessels. The female who was the anesthesiologist had in fact made the comments the patient had heard. At some point after that she reported being pulled in a tunnel towards a distant light; she heard her grandmother's voice; she saw many dead relatives, all bathed by extremely bright light; told her relatives that she must return to her body (and this life) because she did not wish to leave her children to grow up as orphans and, once she did, however reluctantly, she heard the song the attendants were playing while finishing up the procedure.

The question this event raises is how could the patient have had these experiences while anesthetized, before her body (and her brain) was drained of blood and afterwards, when her brain had been rendered inactive and, once again, while anesthetized towards the end? She could, those who believe the NDEs to be products of the brain, would say, because there is no way of excluding the possibility that, though anesthetized, she was aware of her environment—a situation that it is known to arise from time to time—that would account for her veridical perceptions. As for her out-of-body-experience, it is also a known hallucination that can be experimentally produced, as it will be explained later, as probably were her visions of tunnels and dead relatives and lights—products of a brain stressed to an extraordinary degree.

It is certainly impossible to claim that these visions were experienced while the brain of the patient was definitely not functioning, since it is impossible to time precisely when she experienced the visions she later recalled and reported. All these are reasonable propositions. What is unreasonable, however, is to avoid noticing that under circumstances like those described above, as well as other, similar ones, the contention that extremely compromised brains are able of weaving such clear and elaborate experiences, whether true visions or delusions, strains credulity.

Especially so in view of the fact that those that indulge in such explanations believe (along with all experts in these matters) that much slighter brain insults may render people incapable of producing any conscious experience, whatsoever. And the incredible inadequacy of such explanatory hypotheses becomes more obvious the more we examine them with the same critical eye we examine the claim that all these visions constitute evidence of a soul existing and functioning without a brain.

The hypotheses that "explain" these curious experiences form two types of theories: psychological and physiological. Both types have the same structure as those that "explain" mystical experiences as well, resting, as they do, on the materialist or physicalist or Democritean, as I have called it, worldview and, more specifically, on the current neurophysiological model according to which brain events produce experiences.

The psychological theories in the case of NDEs (as in the case of mystical states that will be discussed in chapters 4–6) are entirely inadequate in that the explanations they provide for the phenomena are mere similes and metaphors that require disambiguation and explanation themselves. Consequently, they do no more than obscure the phenomena by referring them either to other phenomena that must in turn be explained, or to hypothetical psychological mechanisms that lie well beyond empirical verification.

For example, there is the psychological theory of "expectation" according to which beliefs about the netherworld create the visions found in NDEs. Expectation, meanwhile is itself a psychological phenomenon the mechanism of which is tacitly hypothesized to be activated by the expectation of imminent death! As for the bliss and love that attends NDEs, well, these are said to be products of psychological "coping mechanisms" in the face of annihilation of the self which begs the question: How would such coping mechanisms evolve since they have no survival value?

Then there is the theory of the "universal memory of birth", that accounts for the tunnel and the light as its end, a completely unverifiable memory and one that leaves out of consideration all the other features of the phenomenon and has no explanatory power whatever for NDEs that do not involve tunnels and lights—and most of them do not. Equally inadequate is the also psychological theory of depersonalization and of other dissociative reactions in response to the stress of impending death. In fact, not a single one of them explains how the psychological state of expectation or of depersonalization or the birth memory act as efficient causes of NDEs, or in what specific way they may produce the varying constellations of visions and sentiments that characterize each NDE.

The physiological theories do not fare any better but for a slightly different reason: without exception, they refer the NDEs (same as they do with the mystical experiences) not to a plausible mechanism of their production, that is, to an efficient cause, but to one or two (actual or hypothetical) conditions among many that might be necessary for their production. In that, they are analogous to the claim that the phenomenon of the movement of a car is explained by the fact that car engines feature spark plugs. In that spirit, "anoxia" is what accounts for NDEs, Blackmore, for example[87], informs us, ignoring, meanwhile, that 100 percent of cardiac arrest patients have anoxia, but not all have NDEs and that non of the NDE cases resulting from expectation of death have anoxia although they have the experience. She also bypasses entirely (as does Blanke[88] who reduces out-of body experiences to the stimulation of a spot in the temporo-parietal junction, and as do all physiological theorists) the issue of how anoxia, or endorphins, or stimulation of a brain spot either alone or in combination create the complex constellation of conscious, lucid and compelling experiences such as the NDEs or the mystical experiences or any other experiences true or delusional, whatsoever.

Therefore, no, we do not have any credible neurophysiological or psychological model for the production of NDEs. Tacit acceptance of the opposite notwithstanding, identification of one of the many antecedent conditions of a phenomenon does not constitute a model of its production. An antecedent condition may be part of the mechanism of the production of a phenomenon but not the mechanism itself. Antecedent conditions are not efficient causes. However, that basic epistemic distinction never dawns on those who struggle to reduce NDEs and mystical states to one or two physiological variables. But even if (or when) a viable working model of how particular experiences are produced by brain mechanisms is proposed, we will still be at a loss to answer the question of whether those parts of NDEs that involve otherworldly visions are veridical or delusional, for reasons that will be discussed in detail in chapter 5, below. Meanwhile, we must return to the main question that was to be settled in this section: are NDEs mystical experiences?

Raymond Moody[89] would have us believe that they are. In his epoch-making book quoted at the beginning of this section, he is claiming that NDEs are ineffable, inexpressible: Many people, he writes, have told him that "There are just no words to express what I am trying to say" or "They just don't make adjectives and superlatives to describe this (NDE)" p. 16. Yet unlike the mystics that struggle, many times in vain, to express their mystical experience, seldom one encounters the same perplexity in the hundreds or narratives of those that have lived through an NDE to describe it. All one has to do to ascertain this truth is to hear the living voice of people like Eben Alexander[90] or Mary Neal[91], both surgeons, describing with confidence the unambiguous visions and sentiments that

87 Blackmore S. Dying to live: Near Death Experience. Buffalo, NY: Prometheus, 1993.
88 Blanke O, Ortigue S, LandisTh.and Seeck M Stimulating illusory own-body perceptions Nature Brief communications. 2002, 419 (19) SEPTEMBER pp 269-270.
89 Moody R A life after life Mokingbird Books, 1975.
90 see e.g. https://www.youtube.com/watch?v=qbkgj5J91hE among others.
91 see e.g. https://www.youtube.com/watch?v=63wY2fylJD0 among others.

comprised their own NDEs. These visions and sentiments may indeed be strange and unexpected but unexpected for their clarity and intensity and not for their obscurity and ineffability.

NDE narratives are like the clear yet otherworldly fiction of Garcia Marques or the canvases of Dali, which are perfectly describable using the ordinary and conventional linguistic and conceptual categories, and not like the ineffable, unitary states, that is, states free of specific perceptual content which, for the Hindu mystics, for Plotinus, Eckhart, Dionysius, the Buddha and the Athonites (as well as for William James, W. T. Stace and all other commentators) are the truly mystical ones. The latter, to quote the philosopher Wainwright, "although are noetic, or perception—like, they are not experiences of specific items within the phenomenal world but intuitive apprehensions of the character of the space-time world as a whole or of something which transcends it" p. 1[92].

In contrast, the phenomenal world of the NDE visions is, verbally, perfectly specifiable, and it is made up of highly specific contents of superlative clarity, or so it seems to this author reading the testimony or listening to the narratives of the people that have experienced them. Therefore, I am forced to conclude that pregnant with meaning and promising to amend our current neurophysiological models of how experiences are engendered, as the NDEs may be, they cannot be considered mystical. They do not possess, in my opinion, the most essential features of all mystical states.

The Mystical Tradition in Judaism and Islam

As it has been mentioned more than once, the peculiar sense of union with God, reported by the mystics, conflicts not only with Christian dogma but also with the teachings of Judaism and Islam. In the case of Judaism, there is a relative paucity of descriptions of mystical experiences whether extrovertive or ecstatic unless one is to interpret visions like that of Moses of the burning bush or Elija's as instances of the former[93]. But one does not need to force on the biblical texts any such interpretations for the purpose of demonstrating the trans-cultural similarities of the mystical experience.

In contrast, the mystical tradition has always been vital in Islam especially among the Sufis where the same prohibitions against the concept or the declaration of essential unity between the human soul and God apply with greater severity. Yet the confession of such unions abounds, as do the descriptions of the experience itself—very similar to those

92 Wainwright W J. Mysticism: A study of its nature, Cognitive Value and Moral Implications. Sussex: The Harvester Press, 1981.

93 See Stace, WT. The teachings of the mystics. New York: Mentor Books, 1960, p. 222.

of mystics of other religions. Also abundant and obvious are the signs of the influence of particular theological dogmas in the description of the experience. This is how Ziyad B. al Arabi (9th century) describes it: "He who is veiled from ecstasy and dominated by the claims of the self, is hampered by making a living and by worldly motives, for the self is veiled by such motives. But if these are banished and devotion to God is made pure from self-interest and the heart comes to itself again and is made refined and pure and gains benefit from exhortation, when it worships God and utters prayers in intimate converse with Him, drawing near to Him, and He addresses it and it hears with attention Him Who speaks, and is contemplating Him and its conscience is pure, then it beholds from what it was freed and there is ecstasy, because it has found what was lost.

Ecstasy in this world comes not from revelation, but consists in the vision of the heart and realization of the truth and gaining assurance, and he who has attained to it beholds with the joy of certainty and with a devotion free of self-interest, for he is all-attentive. When he awakes from the vision, he loses what he has found, but his knowledge remains with him, and for a long time his spirit enjoys that, with the increase of certainty, which he has gained through the vision. This depends upon the servant's proximity to his Lord, or his distance from Him, and upon the vision given to him by his Creator.

But if anyone asks for a further description of ecstasy let him cease to do that, for how can a thing be described which has no description but itself, and no witness to it but itself, and its reality is known from itself, to him who has it: he knows of its existence from his ecstasy. He who does not know it, denies its existence and both he who knows it and he who does not know it are altogether unable to deal with the matter" pp. 20–21[94].

Aware perhaps of the dogmatic prohibitions the mystic names his experience "beholding", not "uniting" or becoming identical with God. Also, the experience is not a gift of the grace of God—it does not come from revelation. In the same spirit, the Persian polymath Ibn Sina, known in the West as Avicenna (about 980–1037) describes in detail the ascending levels of the experience, in a manner similar to that of St. Teresa:

"There are stages and degrees in the contemplative life, to which the gnostic alone in this world attains. The first step for the gnostic is called Will, which means certainty as to the Way. Through this the gnostic will discipline his soul, through his faith, and will direct it towards God, so that he may attain the joy of union. The second stage is that of self-discipline, which is directed towards three things, removing all save God from the Gnostic's (i.e. the mystic's) choice, subduing his carnal

94 Smith, M. Readings from the Mystics of Islam. London: Luzac & Company, Ltd., 1950.

soul to his rational soul, so that the imagination and intellect shall be attracted to the higher things, not the lower, and making the conscience mindful of admonition. The third stage means that the soul, now free from sensual desires, is filled with good thoughts and gives itself up to the spiritual love which seeks to be ruled by the qualities of the Beloved. Now appear to the gnostic flashes of the Divine Light, like fleeting gleams of lightning, which pass away. By those who experience them, these are called 'mystic states' and every state brings joy and becomes more frequent, as the gnostic is more able to receive them. In the fourth stage the mystic sees God in all things and then in the fifth stage he becomes accustomed to God's Presence, the brief flashes of lightning become a shining flame, and he attains to direct knowledge of God and is continually in fellowship with Him"[95].

In contrast, another Persian mystic Abu Yazid al Bistami (804–874), overlooks the dogmatic prohibition and declares the experience to be one of union with God: "I attained the stage of annihilation in God. Nothing is better for Man than to be without aught, having no asceticism, no theory, no practice. When he is without all he is with all"[96]. His conviction that God was within his soul led him to declare "Glory to me! How great is my Majesty". He was, according to Stace[97] among the first "intoxicated" Sufis.

Half a century later, another mystic, Al Hallaj equally intoxicated by the overwhelming potency of his mystical experience of union with God declared "I am the Truth"[98] which was taken by the Islamic authorities to mean "I am God" for which blasphemy, as previously mentioned, he was crucified.

If it were not for the non-intended mystical experiences commented on in the first section of this chapter, it would seem that the mystical experience is a type of religious one whether pantheistic or theistic. It may seem less so when we consider next the drug-facilitated experiences. The purpose, of course, is not to settle the issue of whether the mystical experiences are religious or not, but to determine if there is sufficient justification to consider the latter phenomenologically the same as the former, as Stace, among others did[99] or different as Arthur Koestler, among others, believed[100].

95 In Stace, WT. The teachings of the mystics. New York: Mentor Books, 1960, pp.206-207.
96 Ibid, p. 205.
97 Ibid, 201.
98 Ibid, 202.
99 Smith, H. Cleansing the Doors of Perception: the religious significance of entheogenic plants and chemicals. Boulder CO: Sentient Publications, 2000, p. 24.
100 Koestler A. Return from Nirvana. Sunday Telegraph. March 12, 1961.

3 Mystical States achieved through Psychedelics

The Origins, Classical, and Contemporary Use of Psychedelics

On the Origin of the Belief in a Hidden World

Are, then, the experiences attained through purification, meditation and bodily discipline the same as those that are facilitated by drugs? There is a theory, shared by many, that could be interpreted as implying that it can hardly be otherwise. Mystical experiences, according to that theory, attained through the psychological methods as described in the previous chapter, are essentially due to neurophysiological changes in the brain, no matter how these may have come about.

Ancient people, the theory goes, would have no reason and no real possibilities in their rough daily struggle for survival to conjure up a hidden world, more real than the conventional one, a benevolent world, featuring a loving God and disembodied immortal souls nor to create deliberately a state of mind in which the conventional world seems transfigured by the internal light that beautifies the most humble objects of perception and overwhelms one with bliss. How could they have even tried, if they had no idea what state of mind to be looking for? What happened instead, the theory goes, is that, at some point or other, a few lucky ones found out what is worth looking for—much more worthy, in fact, than anything else. And they found out in two ways.

The first way was by means of a chance encounter with psychotropic plants. It is recounted succinctly by R. Gordon Wasson, the famous ethnobotanist[1], and will be presented below. The second way, the one suggested by Huxley (see below) was through the effects of the inadvertent misery and the pain of their daily travails. In both cases the circumstances are thought to have changed the brain chemistry in that highly specific way that is just right for such an otherworldly state as the mystical, to emerge. And, once the few lucky individuals came upon that fabulous state, they made it their life's priority to rationalize it, to build a religious or philosophical ontology around it, and to seek it fervently thereafter: "As man

1 New York banker and pioneer researcher of the effects of psychoactive plants.

emerged from his brutish past, thousands of years ago", Wasson, writes, "there was a stage in the evolution of his awareness when the discovery of a mushroom (or was it a higher plant?) with miraculous properties was a revelation to him, a veritable detonator to his soul, arousing in him sentiments of awe and reverence, and gentleness and love, to the highest pitch of which mankind is capable, all those sentiments and virtues that mankind has ever since regarded as the highest attribute of his kind. It made him see what this perishing mortal eye cannot see" p. 33[2]. The hidden world and, along with it, God was thus first discovered. For that reason, it is only fitting that the mushrooms and other plants or manufactured substances that revealed Him should be called entheogens. Moreover, this being the case, the criterion of the authenticity of subsequent mystical states, no matter how attained, would necessarily be the phenomenology of the original one that was discovered accidentally.

The second way in which humanity came around to discovering the hidden reality is told by the master storyteller, Aldous Huxley: "For almost half of every year, our ancestors ate no fruit, no green vegetables and (since it was impossible for them to feed more than a few oxen, cows, swine and poultry during the winter months) very little butter or fresh meat, and very few eggs. By the beginning of each successive spring, most of them were suffering, mildly or acutely, from scurvy, due to lack of vitamin C, and pellagra, caused by a shortage in their diet of the B complex. The distressing physical symptoms of these diseases are associated with no less distressing psychological symptoms"[3]. Moreover, "The first result of an inadequate diet is a lowering of the efficiency of the brain as an instrument for biological survival. The undernourished person tends to be afflicted by depression, hypochondria, and feelings of anxiety. He is also liable to see visions... This distress was apt to tinge with its own dark coloring the visionary material, admitted to consciousness through a cerebral valve whose efficiency had been impaired by underfeeding. But in spite of their preoccupations with eternal punishment and in spite of their disease, spiritually minded ascetics often saw heaven and might even be aware, occasionally, of that divinely impartial One, in which the polar opposites are reconciled. For a glimpse of beatitude, for a foretaste of unitive knowledge, no price seemed too high. Mortification of the body may produce a host of undesirable mental symptoms; but it may also open a door into a transcendental world of Being, Knowledge, and Bliss. That is why, in spite of its obvious disadvantages, almost all aspirants to the spiritual life have, in the past, undertaken regular courses of bodily

2 "The Wasson road to Eleusis". In Wasson RG, Hoffmann A and Ruck CA. The Road to Eleusis. Berkeley: North Atlantic Books. (Thirtieth anniversary Edition), 2008.

3 Huxley A. the Doors of Perception and Heaven and Hell. Harper Perennial modern Classics, 1954. (Appendix II).

mortification... Fasting was not the only form of physical mortification resorted to by the earlier aspirants to spirituality. Most of them regularly used upon themselves the whip of knotted leather or even of iron wire. These beatings were the equivalent of fairly extensive surgery without anaesthetics, and their effects on the body chemistry of the penitent were considerable. Large quantities of histamine and adrenalin were released while the whip was actually being plied; and when the resulting wounds began to fester (as wounds practically always did before the age of soap), various toxic substances, produced by the decomposition of protein, found their way into the bloodstream. But histamine produces shock, and shock affects the mind no less profoundly than the body. Moreover, large quantities of adrenalin may cause hallucinations, and some of the products of its decomposition are known to induce symptoms resembling those of schizophrenia. As for toxins from wounds - these upset the enzyme systems regulating the brain, and lower its efficiency as an instrument for getting on in a world where the biologically fittest survive. This may explain why the Cure'd'Ars[4] used to say that, in the days when he was free to flagellate himself without mercy, God would refuse him nothing. In other words, when remorse, self-loathing, and the fear of hell release adrenalin, when self-inflicted surgery releases adrenalin and histamine, and when infected wounds release decomposed protein into the blood, the efficiency of the cerebral reducing valve is lowered and unfamiliar aspects of Mind-at-Large—including psi phenomena, visions, and, if he is philosophically and ethically prepared for it, mystical experiences—will flow into the ascetic's consciousness"[5].

The point of course is not whether histamine or adrenaline or the "decomposed proteins in the blood" constitute the peculiar to the mystical state chemical change in the brain. The point is that some chemical change is produced by starvation and by somatic stress and pain which, in particular settings, gives rise to the mystical state in the consciousness of individuals with particular proclivities and personalities. Then, having made the association between them and the awesome mental state they bring about, the lucky individual systematizes, rationalizes and ritualizes their use and invites others to partake in the ritual.

Does the theory sketched thus far makes it plausible that Plotinus' or a Zen master's mystical experiences are the same as those of Wasson's hypothetical peyote eater as well as those of the Cure'd'Ars who attained them through self-inflicted injuries? Plausible, perhaps. But even if it were true that humanity's mythologies, religions and philosophies—to the degree that they concern a hidden world—have their origins in such

4 St. Jean-Baptiste-Marie Vianney, a Saint of the Roman Catholic Church (1786–1859).

5 Huxley, A. the Doors of Perception and Heaven and Hell. Harper Perennial modern Classics, 1954. (Appendix II).

accidental attainments of the mystical state; even if it were also true that the mystical experiences thus attained are the prototype against which deliberately sought experiences must be compared to verify their authenticity, the similarity of the two sets would still have to rest on the *felt* similarity of the mystical states themselves. Their similarity or difference could not depend on the purely conjectural similarity of the corresponding chemical states of the brain for reasons that will be explained below, in chapter 5.

The Classical Psychedelics

Although a complete description of what constitutes a genuine experience has yet to be given, it has at least been said that it differs radically from visions and apparitions. Such visions do sometimes occur in the process of meditation leading to a mystical experience and sometimes make it difficult to separate them from authentic mystical experiences of the extrovertive variety, as it has been mentioned previously. But what is occasional in the case of meditation is nearly ubiquitous in the case of drug-facilitated experiences.

I should remind the reader here of a point already made in the introductory chapter, namely that visions are not hallucinations but pseudo-hallucinations in that the person knows that they are mental images and do not correspond to things existing in the environment. Such pseudo-hallucinations are the hallmark of ingestion of psychedelic drugs whether or not the ingestion also facilitates the emergence of a mystical state. And, as it has also been mentioned in the introduction, they differ from ordinary mental images in that they seem to be produced without any conscious intention or guidance. In some cases, they are replaced by the authentic mystical state and they reappear once that state begins to abate, thus bracketing it as the slopes of a hill bracket its peak.

In the typical psychedelic experience some somatic changes, sometimes subtle and at other times very pronounced, make their appearance first, accompanied by sensory distortions like "heaving walls" and synesthesias and then by intense visual imagery with a life of its own, where the person feels like a spectator. The resulting sense of suspension of one's will that also characterizes the genuine mystical state makes the distinction between visions and mystical experiences difficult.

Another common element is the affective tone that attends both visions and mystical experiences. Visions can be beatific and blissful or hellish and terrifying. So can the mystical states. But, though difficult, the differentiation of visions from mystical experiences can be made with reasonable degree of certainty. Voluntary control over the genuine mystical experience can sometimes be exerted but at the cost of interfering with it. Similarly, manipulation of drug-induced visions is a strenuous and not always a successful exercise as it is illustrated in the following description of Arthur Koestler's drug-facilitated experience, which is typical in many respects including the fact that it did not develop into a genuine mystical state, as is quite often the case.

"When I closed my eyes I saw luminous, moving patterns of great beauty, which was highly enjoyable; then the patterns changed into planaria kind of flatworm which I had watched under the microscope the previous day in another laboratory; but the worms had a tendency to change into dragons, which was less enjoyable, so I walked out of the show simply by opening my eyes. Then I tried it again, this time directing the beam of the table-lamp, which had a strong bulb, straight at my closed eyelids, and the effect was quite spectacular—rather like the explosive paintings of schizophrenics or Walt Disney's Fantasia. A flaming eddy, the funnel of a tornado, appeared over my head, drawing me upward; with a little auto-suggestion and self-dramatization I could have called it a vision of myself as the prophet Elijah being taken to Heaven by a whirlwind. But 1 felt that this was buying one's visions at the cheap ('Carter's little mushrooms are the Best, mystic experience guaranteed or money refunded'); so I again walked out of the Show by forcing my eyes to open. It was as simple as that...." although it is not always that simple or the visions as innocuous as the following segment from the same report shows:

"The signaling tape recorder was the first symptom of a chemically induced state of insanity. The full effect came on with insidious smoothness and suddenness. Dr. P. came into the room, and a minute or two later I saw the light and realized what a fool I had been to let myself be trapped by his cunning machinations. For during that minute or two he had undergone an unbelievable transformation. It started with the color of his face, which had become a sickly yellowish brown... He stood in a corner of the room with his back to the green wall, and as I stared at him his face split into two, like a cell dividing. It oscillated for a while, then reunited into a single face, and by this time the transformation was complete. A small scar on the Doctor's neck, which I had not noticed before, was gaping wide... one ear had shrunk, the other had grown by several inches, and the face became a smirking, evil phantasm. Then it changed again, into a different kind of Hogarthian vision, and these transformations went on for what I took to be several minutes. All this time the doctor's body remained unchanged, the hallucinations[6] were confined to the space from the neck upward; and they were strongly two-dimensional, like faces cut out of cardboard. The phenomenon was always strongest in that corner of the room where it had first occurred and faded into less offensive distorting-mirror effects when we moved elsewhere, although the lighting of the room was uniform. The same happened when other

6 The proper term should have been pseudo-hallucinations since he was aware of the fact they were such.

members of the staff joined us later. One of them, the jovial Dr. F., was transformed into a vision so terrifying—a Mongol with a broken neck hanging from an invisible gallows—that I thought I was going to be sick; yet I could not stop myself staring at him. We stood face to face in the 'evil corner', and with my pupils dilated by the drug I must have looked unpleasant, for he asked in an embarrassed voice: 'Why are you staring at me so?' In the end, I said: 'For God's sake let's snap out of it', and we moved into another part of the room, where the effect became much weaker. As the last remark indicates, I was still in control of my outward behaviour, and this remained true throughout the whole three or four hours of the experience. But at the same time I had completely lost control over my perception of the world. I made repeated efforts 'to walk out of the show' as I had been able to do during the first stages on the couch, but I was powerless against the delusions. I kept repeating to myself: 'But these are nice, friendly people, they are your friends, and so on'. It had no effect whatsoever on the spontaneous and inexorable visual transformations. At one stage, these spread from the faces of others to my own right hand which shriveled into a cripple's, and to the metal bars of the table lamp, which were transformed into the claws of a predatory bird. Then I asked for a mirror to be brought in, expecting to see a picture of Dorian Gray. Strangely enough, there was no change in my own face"[7].

Though unable to inhibit his visual imagery Koestler was throughout aware that it was his "show" and it did not reflect conventional reality. Incidentally, this experience (that did not evolve into a mystical one) contributed to his doubt that the genuine mystical state can be attained with the aid of drugs. Another subtle point of difference between visions and mystical states is that although both can evoke intense positive or negative affect, the quality of the two differs substantially. How visions like those described by Koestler in the quotation above can be terrifying needs no further elaboration. But the negative affect of the authentic mystical state whether drug-facilitated or not, is of a quite different kind. In the words of Gordon Wasson, "...at last you know what ecstasy means. Ecstasy! For the Greeks, *ekstasis* meant the flight of the soul from the body. Can you find a better word than that to describe the bemushroomed state? In common parlance ecstasy is fun. But ecstasy is not fun. Your very soul is seized and shaken until it tingles. Who will choose to feel undiluted awe, or to float through that door yonder into the Divine Presence?" p. 162[8].

The affective valence of the visions, which, once again, are not part of the mystical experience, does not appear to depend on the psychotropic drug but on how the physiological and cognitive effects of it are assimilated

7 Koestler, A. Return from Nirvana. Sunday Telegraph. March 12,1961.

8 Wasson, RG. Soma: Divine mushroom of immortality. New York: Harcourt Brace Jovanovich, 1968/1971.

in the consciousness of the individual. The manner of that assimilation, in turn, seems to depend on two factors: the personality of the individual including, as it does, his psychological past, and the circumstances or the context in which he experiences the visions or, in the vernacular of the psychedelic culture, on the *set* and the *setting*.

People who for one reason or other have difficulty relinquishing control over their sensations and perceptions are likely to panic if they realize that they cannot exercise absolute control of "the show"—as Koestler called it, or when they fear the changes they feel in their physiological state, even if they know in advance that such changes may happen. And, the panic can snowball into a crisis of the kind that has sent thousands of recreational drug users to the hospital in the 60s and early 70s to deal with their "*bad trips*".

Moreover, the fact that sometimes the "shows" cannot be stopped, can become unpleasant even to people that are otherwise free of psychological problems. This is where the setting, mainly the presence of others who can reassure those having the visions by reminding them, for example, that the unpleasant situation is reversible, and that they are not "losing their mind" is important in averting the transformation of an unpleasant feeling into a feeling or terror.

The fact that the *set* and the *setting* are so important in determining the nature of the mystical experience has sometimes led people to minimize the essential role of the drugs in the elicitation of the mystical experience. But the character of an aspiring mystic and the circumstances, however favorable for the elicitation of a mystical state, can never match the dependability of such elicitation that the drugs provide. The attainment of the state depends on the drugs much like the attainment of a percept depends on the presence of an ambiguous object while the personality and the expectations of the mystic condition the nature of the mystical state much like the visual acuity and the expectations of a perceiver condition the nature of the percept.

Psychedelics come in many varieties. Those that are most frequently used—the so-called "classical" psychedelics—are primarily, though not exclusively, serotonin agonists, that is they bind to serotonin receptors, mainly the receptor 5-HT 2A. This is known because serotonin antagonists, that is, chemicals that block the effects of serotonin also block the effects of these psychotropic drugs.

On the basis of their chemical structure, the classic psychedelics are divided into two classes. The one includes drugs with a chemical structure like that of tryptamine. Among the drugs in this class are the synthesized psychedelic LSD, psilocybin, and dimethyltryptamine or DMT, which is found in ayahuasca, a psychotropic concoction used ritually in South America. The second category includes substances with a chemical structure similar to phenethylamine. Mescaline, the main psychoactive agent in the peyote (Lophophora williamsii), and other cacti, is the best-known psychedelic of that class. This class includes also several synthesized compounds. The cactus Peyote has been used for millennia by several Mexican Indian tribes including the Chichimeca, Huichol, and Tarahumara tribes, for therapeutic and religious purposes[9] and it continues to be used today as a sacrament by the Native American Church to be recounted below.

Psilocybin (4-phosphoryloxy-N,N-dimethyltryptamine), is contained in mushrooms of the genus Psilocybe that are found on all continents. It has also been used in the context of rituals by American Indian tribes in Mexico for centuries and it is used today in the context of formal experiments and studies of its psychotherapeutic efficacy in several university laboratories in Europe and North America.

DMT (N,N-dimethyltryptamine) is yet another tryptamine alkaloid that has been used in South America for therapeutic and religious purposes for many centuries[10]. As mentioned above, it is one basic ingredient in ayahuasca which is made by plants that are rich in it as well as plants that contain monoamine oxidase inhibitors or MOIs—the familiar antidepressant medication.

The critical importance of the *set* and the *setting* in addition to that of the psychotropic drugs must have been appreciated since the earliest experimentation with such substances, because, in the past, they have been used exclusively in the context of medicinal or religious rituals where the practitioners' reactions and the setting could be appropriately controlled. The earliest use of psychotropic substances goes back thousands of years. In the next sections, I will briefly describe three examples of such use where there is enough evidence with which to construct a reasonably informative picture as to what the effects of these substances were.

Ritualistic use of Psychedelics: Three Examples

Among the gods that the Aryans brought with them in India four millennia ago, one, called *soma* in Rig Veda[11] is peculiar, in that it was a plant that when consumed, it was said to confer on those that consumed him Immortality: "we have drunk Soma and become immortal"[12]. The identity of this botanical god was until recently a mystery in part because after the 9th century BC its use was abandoned. But it must have been an important god because of the one thousand and twenty-eight hymns contained in Rig Veda one hundred and fourteen are dedicated to him[13].

9 Schultes RE, Hofmann A and Ratsch C. Plants of the Gods: their sacred, healing, and hallucinogenic powers. Healing Arts Press. 2001.

10 Ibid.

11 One of the four Vedas, the ancient Sanskrit scriptures of the Hindu religion. Each Veda has four parts. The Upanishads form the fourth part.

12 Smith, H. Cleansing the Doors of Perception: the religious significance of entheogenic plants and chemicals. Boulder CO: Sentient Publications, 2000. p. 49.

13 Ibid.

In these hymns, this botanical God is never said to possess any of the typical colors of plants such as green, or gray, but instead, it is described as red and as white. There is no mention of its having leaves, roots, flowers and no mention of its baring fruits. But there is reference to its stem and to its cap and to its golden-colored juice—when it was pressed. Its hide, the hymns say, is a bull and its dress is sheep and it wraps himself in brilliant cloth that is like a cloud. Moreover, he sheds or abandons his envelop and like a snake creeps out of his skin. When eaten, he alters consciousness but unlike alcohol, it does not have any ill effects; instead, it leads to godliness. Its effects are summarized in one of the hymns as follows:

> "We have drunk the Soma
> we have become immortal
> we have arrived at the light
> we have found the gods
> what can now the enemy do to harm us
> and what malice can mortals entertain?
> Amplify, O Soma, our lives
> For the purpose of living"[14]

The same effects, Rig Veda informs us, are experienced by those that drink the urine of the people that had consumed the god—a practice also known in Siberia and other places. This implies that the psychotropic agent is not metabolized—a property that as Gordon Wasson[15] realized, was that of musicimol, the psychotropic principle in a mushroom named Amanita Muscaria or, commonly, fly agaric, found in Europe and Asia. That mushroom also has the effects described in the above-quoted hymn, when ingested; and does rupture from its embryonic envelope like a snake shedding its skin; and does have a white stem the color of sheep and a red cap—the color of favored bulls in India—and no, it has neither flowers nor leaves.

The clues thus interpreted by Wasson led to the identification of the mystery god in the late 60s[16]. His solution of the old riddle may not have the persuasive force of a mathematical proof but it did convince most of the commentators that responded to his publication, including several eminent Sanskrit scholars, botanists, like Richard Schultes of the Harvard Botanical Museum, anthropologists like Levi-Straus of the Collège de France and Linguists like Roman Jacobson.

But whether or not Wasson's identification of the Amanita Muscaria as the legendary Soma is correct, the point here is that this psychotropic agent, whatever it may be exactly, facilitated the type of experience that

14 Ibid p. 56.
15 Wasson, RG. Soma: Divine mushroom of immortality. New York: Harcourt Brace Jovanovich, 1968/1971.
16 Ibid.

generations of Indian visionaries and yogis after the 9th century BC are trying, to this day, to recapture through meditation and other techniques of psychophysiological control. Granted, there is no guarantee that the experiences occasionally attained through these techniques are identical to those facilitated by Soma. But to the degree that the phenomenological description goes, they are similar enough.

The same sort of evidence suggests the possibility that the notion common in early Western philosophy and most explicitly in Plato, of a hidden world of disembodied souls and eternal forms, of which our conventional world is a poor copy, emerged not as a logical inference from axioms and theorems but as a revelation; in fact, as a drug-facilitated revelation in the context of a religious ceremony. The reason for this assertion is that Plato's language, when describing the hidden order of his ontology, is almost identical with that used by mystics of all traditions to describe the object of their mystical experience, including the quality of the visions which, as previously mentioned, bracket that experience.

Since there is no evidence that he attained mystical knowledge by the dialectical method he describes in the Symposium (see the third section of chapter 2, above) and since, on the contrary, there is every reason to believe that he was initiated in the Eleusinian mysteries, it is conjectured that he attained the knowledge he is describing as it was revealed to him at Eleusis[17]. His descriptions apposed to those known to have been inspired by psychotropic substances bear this out: Who would praise the beauty of the straight line or of a patch of plain white color as Plato does in this passage from Philebus[18] if not someone who saw them with the eyes of an initiate in some Mysteries, empowered by some psychotropic substance or other?

"...when I say beauty of (geometrical forms) I am not trying to say what most people would mean by such expressions as 'the beauty of animals or that of some paintings' but...the straight line and the circle...because the beauty of those (simple) things is not relative like that of other (compound) things but they are always beautiful in themselves and they are associated with their own set of pleasures.... 51 C-D"[19] And Huxley seconds him: "I looked down by chance....at my own crossed legs. Those folds of the trousers....how rich, how deeply, mysteriously sumptuous!"[20].

Plato, again, describing the earth of the other, the hidden world: "...it is divided into sectors of different colors of which the colors here are mere patches in a painter's palate. But there the entire earth is covered with them and they are much more bright and pure than those here with one sector

17 A town in Attica, a short distance from Athens, the seat of the Eleusinian Mysteries, an annual celebration of the Greek and later, the Greco-Roman world.

18 One of the late Platonic Dialogues.

19 Plato, Philebus.

20 Huxley, A. the Doors of Perception and Heaven and Hell. Harper Perennial modern Classics, 1954.p. 30.

being a purple of wondrous beauty, another golden and another white, whiter than chalk or snow...and the mountains and stones are smoother and more translucent and the colors more beautiful ... 110 C-E"[21].

But, perhaps more tellingly, when the souls went in the other world, awaiting their next incarnation, "they beheld beauty shining bright...and the blessed sights and visions and were initiated into that which is justly called the most blessed of mysteries...being allowed as initiates to see the simple, serene and blissful apparitions in pure light... 250 B-C"[22].

Of course, it could be purely coincidental that Plato wrote of the other world in the same way as those ancient Hindus who were inspired by Soma, as Huxley inspired by mescaline and as the many parishioners of the American Indian Church and the participants in formal studies today who are inspired by psilocybin. But, I believe, one could doubt that such similarities are merely coincidental without appearing gullible or unreasonable.

Be that as it may, the facilitating substance in the Eleusinian Mysteries was the Kykeon and the ceremonies were annually celebrated in the small town of Eleusis a short distance from Athens. The indications that a psychotropic substance was at the heart of the Mysteries are indirect but highly suggestive. They include descriptions of the physiological effects of kykeon and descriptions of the ineffable experience following its ingestion that match those of the known psychotropic substances as well as those of Soma. Moreover, the rituals preceding induction to the Mysteries and those during them are also matching the moral and psychological preparation of the prospective mystics[23] belonging to the other traditions already reviewed.

Until the publication of the now classic book by the same Wasson who solved the riddle of Soma, and his two co-authors, Albert Hoffmann, the discoverer of LSD and the classicist Carl Ruck, the ineffable, secret, and sacred experiences attained during the last night of the ceremony in Eleusis was attributed, by historians and classicists, to the drama enacted by the hierophant—the high priest of the precinct—and his assistants at the induction night inside the Telesterion—the hall of the ceremonies. Several factors however, all laid out in their book "The Road to Eleusis"[24] render, in retrospect, that explanation quite inadequate. Here is a brief summary of them:

Except for the year 480 BC when the Persian army was occupying Attica, the Mysteries were celebrated every September for fifteen centuries, up to

21 Plato, Phaedo. Translation mine

22 Plato, Phaedrus. Translation mine

23 The original meaning of the term mystic was "the one who shuts his eyes" in readiness to experience the revelation whereas what we mean by mystic today was expressed by the term epoptes, (επόπτης) that is "the surveyor".

24 The Wasson road to Eleusis. In Wasson RG, Hoffmann A and Ruck CA. The Road to Eleusis. Berkeley: North Atlantic Books. (Thirtieth anniversary Edition),1978/2008.

381 AD when, by decree of the emperor of the Eastern Roman Empire, Theodosius, they were abolished, because they were offering an all too serious challenge to the spread and dominion of Christianity. During these centuries thousands of pilgrims from the Hellenic and later the Greco-Roman world, aristocrats and slaves, men and women, philosophers and illiterate folks alike experienced the once in a lifetime[25] sacred state that marked indelibly their lives—much like the authentic mystical experiences continue to do today (see the next two sections). The sheer range of variation of the population of the initiates with dramatically varying backgrounds, coming from cultures that were continuously evolving and changing over the centuries, renders the supposition that all of them would have such an experience simply because they witnessed some sort of drama, enacted by the hierophant and his assistants in the ceremonial hall, highly improbable.

In the first place, a great many of these pilgrims were schooled in theater. Consequently, if the plays of Aeschylus or Euripides were insufficient to induce mystical experiences in them all, it is extremely hard to see how a stereotyped ceremony, however sacred, even as sacred as the Holy Eucharist is for devout Christians today, would accomplish such a miracle. Moreover, the physical design of the Telesterion, a rectangular building very unlike a theater, with a roof supported by a forest of columns that obstruct the view from many angles, would obstruct the view of the dramatic performance for most of the initiates—two to three thousands of them—seated in steps against the four walls of the hall.

Most importantly still, the conventional interpretation of the Mysteries cannot account for the type of experiences that followed upon the drinking of Kykeon, a concoction of barley, mint, water and, possibly, other ingredients. That drink was prepared exclusively from barley cultivated and harvested by one of the two priestly families of Eleusis, a town that formed part of the Athenian State. Upon drinking it, Plutarch tells us[26], "the pilgrims experienced shivering, cold sweat, and vertigo". Then came the revelation that justified belief in the notion of immortality: The initiates beheld "the end of life as well as its divinely granted beginning"[27].

What it was, exactly, that was revealed has never been explained because there was a state law that forbade the mystics from divulging to non-initiated people the content of the revelation on pain of death. The only thing told publically was that what was revealed were the "hiera"—the holy things. If these hiera were objects, relics of some sort, or if they were a pantomime of the religious story of Persephony's abduction to the underworld and her return, most of the pilgrims in the Telesterion would not be able to see them and have a mystical experience because they saw them.

25 The initiates in the mysteries could only participate once.

26 frg. 178 Strobaeus 4. 52. 49 p. 1089.

27 Pindar, fragment 121 (Bowra).

Moreover, the same hiera were profaned by the *enfant terrible* of the 5th century Athens, Alcibiades and his patrician friends, being shown (or enacted) in his and some of his friends' houses during their revels right before the Athenian expedition to Sicily, for which profanation he was indicted[28].

But whatever it was that constituted the hiera, the fact remains that before they were revealed all the initiates had drunk of the Kykeon offered to them by the temple's priestesses. Therefore, the Wasson, Hoffman and Ruck theory goes, the hiera could be the visions associated with psychotropic substances, or, I may add, they could be whatever symbols of the cult the initiates were shown transfigured by the extrovertive, in that case, drug-facilitated, mystical state. The main indications that this may in fact had been the case have already been outlined. As for the Kykeon, it is conjectured that it contained the extract of the parasitic fungus ergot that infests the barley and was allowed to flourish in the fields of the Temple cultivated exclusively, as mentioned, by one of the two priestly families of hierophants. If processed appropriately, ergot could yield sufficient quantities for preparing the Kykeon for the one to three thousand pilgrims every year[29].

The uniformity of the response of the initiated, that is, the epoptae, or the "surveyors" of the things revealed, was also secured by the fact that all of them had gone through the "minor Mysteries" in Athens during the six months preceding the ceremonies. In that time they were purified, and prepared for the main event by becoming familiar with the rites and formulating expectations as to what it was to be revealed to them much like the Christian mystics proceed in the pursuit of the mystical knowledge with definite expectations regarding the object of the experience they are seeking.

If there are doubts as to the role of psychedelics in the Eleusinian Mysteries there is none in the case of the Native American Church. Also, the total lack of individual accounts of the Eleusinian experience is more than made up in the context of that Church's rituals. The Native American Church, a mixture of traditional American Indian beliefs in the Great Spirit and Christian precepts has about a quarter million members and uses peyote as its sacrament.

The Church services, unlike those of the other Christian denominations, are not conducted regularly on Sundays or any other days but only when Church members have a need for them: to celebrate a birth, to mourn a loss, or to seek support in the face of some difficulty or other. Accordingly, the experiences sought and expected by the participants are conditioned by those circumstances.

28 Plutarch, Alcibiades.

29 The Wasson road to Eleusis. In Wasson RG, Hoffmann A and Ruck CA. The Road to Eleusis. Berkeley: North Atlantic Books. (Thirtieth anniversary Edition),1978/2008. p. 151.

The service is conducted either by a priest or an elder who is called a roadman—one who shows the way. It follows an older ritual of the pre-Christian era involving an all-night vigil in a tipi with the congregation sitting around a fire. The focal point of the service is the ingestion of peyote amidst singing of religious songs in anticipation of the transport to the hidden reality, which will alleviate sufferings and intensify joys. An idea of the quality of experience attained may be gleaned by the sample of statements of participants in the rite, quoted below:

"God endowed it (the peyote) with his love and compassion. He put those qualities into this lowly herb so that when we eat it we can feel that the love that the God is—I emphasize the love that God is, not that God has—is physically inside us. From there it overflows in compassion for human beings and all other kinds of creatures. p. 116"[30]. It is worth noting here that the attribute of felt love is characterizing the experiences of all mystics whether drug-facilitated or not: "Chief Peyote tells us that our meetings are to make Indians good. To make them friends, and to make them stop fighting. When we eat Peyote we feel towards others a warm glow in our hearts as if they were our brothers". p. 120[31].

"I have never seen colors or experienced delusions of any sort while taking Peyote. What it feels like is that I am sitting right by God the Creator. I communicate with him., And whatever I pray for, I feel that he hears me" p. 118[32]. This is yet another form of contact of the self with God, besides beholding him or merging with his essence or his energy. The same form of contact with Divinity is expressed in the following quotes:

"In the first creation, God himself used to talk to people and tell them what to do. Long after, Christ came among the white people and told them what to do. Then God gave us Indians Peyote. That's how we found God". p. 118[33]. Or, "There are certain times in a meeting when you can feel a presence. It is a holy feeling the presence of the spirit of God..." p. 119[34].

People lacking the expository talents of a Huxley or a Koestler can only express the cardinal aspects of their experiences and that in much more ambiguous terms than they. This and the fact that the variability in the amount of peyote ingested by each participant and the type of the experience sought in each particular occasion that prompts each service renders the testimony of these mystics less than sufficient to answer the main question pursued in this section, namely whether the drug-facilitated experiences are the same as those attained without the aid of drugs.

30 Smith, H. Cleansing the Doors of Perception: the religious significance of entheogenic plants and chemicals. Boulder CO: Sentient Publications, 2000.

31 Ibid.

32 Ibid.

33 Ibid.

34 Ibid.

To address these inadequacies and attack the question directly was the purpose of the legendary and first formal study of psychedelics known as the "Good Friday experiment" to be discussed in the next section along with other formal investigations that have begun recently, following the hiatus of prohibition of the use of psychotropic substances in the late 60s and early 70s.

The Good Friday Experiment

The, now legendary, Good Friday experiment was conducted by a physician named Walter Pahnke, as part of the requirements for a theology doctorate he was pursuing at Harvard[35]. The essential aspects of the experiment were subsequently replicated with methodological improvements by Ronald Griffiths and his associates[36]. Moreover, the similarity of meditation-induced and drug-facilitated experiences indirectly addressed in the experiments was directly addressed later in a large survey[37] that will also be described below.

The purpose of the Good Friday experiment was to determine whether, with the appropriate set and setting, the classic psychedelic psilocybin given at an adequate dose would facilitate experiences that fulfill the description of genuine mystical ones as defined by the eminent expert in the area, Walter Stace[38], and the degree to which the experience had long-term repercussions in the life of the participants.

Ten pairs of white, male, divinity students—all Protestants, matched closely for religious background, personality and prior religious experiences were selected, thus fulfilling the requirement of the appropriate *set*. One member of each pair was given at random either 30mg of psilocybin or a placebo, nicotinic acid, during the Good Friday services in the basement of the Marsh Chapel of Boston University, itself a smaller chapel while the service was broadcast into it as it was proceeding upstairs in the Main Chapel. This and the fact that the environment was a chapel full of religious symbolism fulfilled the requirement of the appropriate *setting*.

Two assumptions were implicitly made: first, that the religious experience that the set and setting were to engender with the aid of the drug are

35 Pahnke, WN. Drugs and mysticism: An analysis of the relationship between psychedelic drugs and the mystical consciousness. Cambridge, MA: Harvard University Press. 1963.

36 Barrett, FS. and Griffiths, RR. Classic hallucinogens and mystical experiences: Phenomenology and neural correlates. Current Topics in Behavioral Neurosciences, 2017, 430.

37 Griffiths RR, Hurwitz ES, Davis AK, Johnson MW, Jesse R. Survey of subjective "God encounter experiences": Comparisons among naturally occurring experiences and those occasioned by the classic psychedelics psilocybin, LSD, ayahuasca, or DMT. PLoS ONE, 2019, 14(4): e0214377. https://doi.org/10.1371/journal.pone.0214377 Editor: Rosemary Frey, University of Auckland.

38 Stace, WT. Mysticism and Philosophy. London: Macmillan Press, 1960.

the same as all recorded and reported authentic mystical experiences, not involving drugs. The assumption is reasonable given the fact that most if not all mystical experiences reported in the ancient and contemporary literature are in fact religious in content. The second assumption was that the features of authentic experiences that Stace had proposed in his classic publication did in fact capture the essence of such experiences, which, as it will be made apparent in the next section, was an equally cogent assumption.

There were no specific instructions to the twenty participants as to what they were about to experience nor were they told who was given psilocybin and who nicotinic acid to curtail expectancy effects. Soon, however, this became obvious from the behavior of the participants and their verbal interactions (thus vitiating the "blind" aspect of the experimental design) but it did not compromise in any serious way the results of the experiment. At the end of the study, when the drug effects were over, the subjects were asked to what degree their experiences matched Stace's features of either "introvertive" or "extrovertive" unity, "transcendence of time and space", "positive mood", "sense of sacredness", "sense of objectivity and reality" of the experience, "paradoxicality" of the experience, its "ineffability" and its "transiencecy".

Six months later, the long term or persisting changes in the personality and behavior of the participants were also estimated. The way in which the presence of the above-mentioned features of authentic mystical experience and the degree to which they characterized each participant's experience were assessed, was as follows: Each participant recounted his experience and his testimony was transcribed and tape-recorded. Also, each filled out a 147-item questionnaire (and a shorter one six months later). Raters of these testimonies, blind to the details of the experimental design, well versed in "content analysis" procedures scored independently of each other the descriptions of the participants' experiences. These scores along with the participants' responses to the questionnaire were averaged. Each averaged score represented the percentage of maximum possible degree to which each of Stace's mystical features characterized the experience of each participant.

Pahnke decided that average scores of 60–70% of maximum and above were sufficient to classify a participant's experience as mystical. According to this reckoning, four of the ten participants that took psilocybin and none of those who took the placebo (nicotinic acid) were deemed to have attained the mystical state. The conclusion reached in that study was that indeed, the mystical experiences facilitated by the psychedelic drug were similar to mystical experiences attained by other means in that the former were characterized by the same core features as were the latter, according to Stace's specifications.

A second conclusion, useful for the research that followed, was that a sizeable proportion of people are likely to attain the mystical state by the aid of psychedelic drugs thus enabling the collection of reliable data in laboratory contexts were *set* and *setting* and the drug dosages can be controlled, and enhancing our knowledge of the mystical state as well as its sustained effects on people's behavior, affective state and mentation. Clearly, though, that proportion depends on several factors. First, it depends on the numerical criterion of what constitutes a mystical state. Second, it depends on whether the responses of the participants, quantified in the way described above, capture accurately the features of the authentic mystical experience and third, on the degree to which Stace's features, as stated in the study, capture the essence of the mystical experience.

Formal Contemporary Studies with Psychedelics

In subsequent experiments, like the one to be described below, the 60% of maximum score was retained as a criterion because for the practical purpose that most of these studies were (and are) conducted (i.e. the assessment of the therapeutic effects of the psychedelics) the criterion is serviceable and it is now widely used. Moreover, to the degree that the reported experiences in drug studies continue to be recognizably similar to those of mystical states attained without drugs, this issue will not retain us any longer.

The issue of the validity of the measures used in the groundbreaking Good Friday study has been satisfactorily addressed in subsequent experiments as have a number of other shortcomings like its limited generalizability in view of the small and demographically selective sample of participants it employed. But the study was replicated and several of its shortcomings were corrected[39]. An important improvement was the use of standardized and validated scales replacing the methods used in the Good Friday experiment to quantify the participant's experiences, the "Hood Mysticism Scale" and the "Spiritual Transcendence Scale"[40].

Moreover, in contrast with the original Good Friday study instead of nicotinic acid, methylphenidate (Ritalin) was used as placebo because its effects mimic in some ways those of psilocybin and it has a similar time course. Also, the same group of thirty-six participants served in two different conditions: in the experimental (psilocybin) and the placebo condition. Each participant was tested individually; they formed a more representative sample of the population than did the participants in the Good Friday experiment, and were well educated, psychiatrically and medically healthy, and had never used psychedelics before. Authentic or "complete mystical experiences" during psilocybin sessions were attained by 61% of participants—a higher percentage than in the Good Friday

39 Griffiths RR, Richards WA, McCann U, Jesse R. Psilocybin can occasion mystical-type experiences having substantial and sustained personal meaning and spiritual significance. Psychopharmacology (Berl). 2006, 187(3):268–283; discussion 284–292.

40 Other scales have since been constructed and validated—see e.g. Barrett, FS, & Griffiths, RR. Classic hallucinogens and mystical experiences: Phenomenology and neural correlates. Current Topics in Behavioral Neurosciences. 2017, 430—but all of them are ultimately based on the features derived by W T Stace.

study—although the same criterion for a complete mystical experience was used, i.e. a score of 60% of maximum on each dimension of the Mystical Experience Questionnaire.

Two months after the experiment, 71% of the participants rated their experience with the psychedelic substance as among the five most spiritually significant experiences of their lives and 33% as the single most significant, while only an 8% of participants rated the ritalin experience as being among the top five most significant experiences of their lives and no subject rated it as the single most significant event. Over a year later, most participants rated their experiences similarly in terms of importance[41].

Are, therefore, the drug-facilitated mystical states the same as those attained through meditation? On the basis of this study, the answer would be positive, much like in the case of Pahnke's study but obliquely so, since no drug-independent mystical experiences were contrasted to establish the similarity using the same assessment procedures and this only to the degree that Stace's features of the authentic mystical states are correct. But a more recent survey did address the question of similarity directly.

In this online survey[42], prospective participants were informed of the purpose of the study which was worded as follows: "In this survey, we want to characterize various experiences of encounters with something that someone might call: God (e.g., the God of your understanding), Higher Power, Ultimate Reality, or an Aspect or Emissary of God (e.g., an angel)". Responders who had claimed such an encounter with the aid of either psilocybin, LSD, DMT or ayahuasca were included if they were 18 years old or older, they could read, write, and speak English fluently, had not completed the questionnaire previously, and have had an experience involving some aspect of the divinity as described in the purpose statement. Responders who claimed to have had such an experience without the aid of drugs were included if they also met the same demographic criteria.

A total of 809 people that met the criteria were included in the non-drug group, 1184 were included in the psilocybin, 1251 in the LSD, 435 in the ayahuasca, and 606 in the DMT group. They all rated their experiences on-line using a version of the "Mystical Experience Questionnaire" mentioned previously. Of the 3,476 people in all drug groups combined, 64% met the criteria of an authentic or "complete" mystical experience. The percentages for the different psychedelics were 73% for the DMT group, 65% for the ayahuasca, 62% for the psilocybin and 61% for the LSD group.

41 Griffiths RR, Richards W, Johnson M, McCann U, Jesse R. Mystical-type experiences occasioned by psilocybin mediate the attribution of personal meaning and spiritual significance 14 months later. J Psychopharmacology. 2008, 22(6):621–632.

42 Griffiths RR, Hurwitz ES, Davis AK, Johnson MW, Jesse R. Survey of subjective "God encounter experiences": Comparisons among naturally occurring experiences and those occasioned by the classic psychedelics psilocybin, LSD, ayahuasca, or DMT. PLoS ONE. 2019, 14(4): e0214377.

A lower percentage of the 809 non-drug participants, namely 43% met the same criteria. Although it is to be expected that the drug dosages and the settings would vary across the sample, it is remarkable that approximately the same proportion of those participants attained the mystical state as in the above-mentioned well-controlled laboratory experiment. Most participants in all groups who met the criteria of a genuine mystical experience reported that the encounter was with an entity that was "conscious, benevolent, intelligent, sacred, eternal and all-knowing".

Although there were some demographic differences between the no-drug and the drug groups, which were statistically corrected, it would be rather otiose not to conclude that whether mediated by psychedelics or not, the mystical states were in all probability the same. But we will revisit this point later in this section. Needless to say, the similarity concerns the mystical state exclusively and not the occasional physiological and psychological ill effects associated with the ingestion of psychedelics like elevated blood pressure and heart rate, anxiety, nausea, vomiting and headache.

But the survey produced some additional interesting results regarding the long-term effects of the experience, the most impressive being that more than 60% of those that reported they were atheists before their mystical experience became religious as a result of it. Other effects of having had the experience were persisting positive attitudes towards life and a sense of meaning and purpose. Data on positive personality changes and therapeutic effects of the drug-facilitated mystical states have been and continue to accumulate. Although they can hardly be used to answer the question as to the objectivity of the contents of the mystical knowledge, unless one employs the pragmatic criterion of usefulness exclusively[43] they do vouch for the practical value of the mystical state in the day-to-day living, however, attained.

Typical changes in attitudes and lifestyle can be gleaned by the subjective responses of participants in another psilocybin study: "I have an increased commitment to spiritual practices; I think my heart is more open to all interactions with other people; more aware of choices, take time to pause and choose, more breaks; better boundaries at work and personal relationships"[44]. Or "I feel that I relate better in my marriage. There is more empathy—a greater understanding of people and understanding their difficulties and less judgment. Less judging of myself too". Or "A greater integration of the pieces of my life; more spiritless religion; less fear of being wrong". Or "Less concerned with the appearance of 'spirituality',

43 See e.g. William James' on "Pragmatism" and on "The meaning of truth" In William James Writings 1902–1910. Library of America. Literary Classics of the United States, Inc., 1987.

44 Griffiths RR, Johnson MW, Richards WA, Richards BW, McCann U and Robert J. Psilocybin occasioned mystical-type experiences: immediate and persisting dose-related effects. Psychopharmacology. 2011, 218:649–665 p. 662.

while realizing more that everything is sacred. I feel more accommodating and forgiving toward both friends and strangers, and less anxious to label them or convert them to my viewpoint. I am learning to recognize and release old definitions of myself".

As of this day, the therapeutic effects of drug-facilitated mystical states are being evaluated for several diagnostic groups. Summaries of these applications before and after the prohibition of research with psychedelics in the late 60s can be found in a number of reviews[45].

Very briefly, contemporary research on the therapeutic efficacy of psychedelics, mainly psilocybin and LSD but ayahuasca as well, has shown repeatedly efficacy of these psychotropic drugs, sustained over months after a single session, in reducing anxiety and depression symptoms associated with life-threatening cancer, and more specifically, the prospect of dying. The effects have been shown to be mediated by mystical experiences in that they are seeing only in individuals who have attained the mystical state.

The effect is not surprising in view of the fact that one of the features of the mystical state is the certainty it inspires in the indestructibility of consciousness; if not the personal consciousness then the consciousness that is a distinctive feature of the "Presence" encountered in the mystic state. In William Richard's words[46]: "It is of interest that cancer patients and others who find such profound mystical experiences in their memory banks are not necessarily convinced of personal immortality, that is, the continual existence after death of the everyday personality that goes with the common names. 'Life after death' implies a temporal sequence. Rather, they tend to report a conviction that Eternity, or Infinity, a state of consciousness outside of time, is so unquestionably real to them that it does not matter one way or the other whether the everyday personality survives when the body stops functioning and decomposes".

Promising results concerning the reduction of symptoms of depression are also accumulating in studies using DMT-containing ayahuasca and psilocybin. However, no large-scale clinical trials have been completed as of today, although some of the preliminary studies thus far completed show substantial reduction of symptoms, again correlated with the depth of the mystical state attained, as reflected in standardized questionnaire scores.

Much more definite is the evidence for the efficacy of psychedelics in resolving addiction. The first such indications emerged from a meta-analysis of data collected in the 70s and 90s which showed that LSD nearly doubled the odds of abstinence on the part of alcohol addicts. In

45 Johnson MW, Hendricks PS, Barrett FS, Griffiths RR. Classic Psychedelics: An integrative review of epidemiology, mystical experience, brain network function, and therapeutics. 2018, https://doi.org 10.1016/j.pharmthera. 2018.11.010; Rucker JH, Iliff J and Nutt DJ. Psychiatry & the psychedelic drugs. Past, present & future. Neuropharmacology. 2018, 142 200–218; Nichols DE Psychedelics. Pharmacological Reviews. 2016, 266–355

46 Richards W A. Sacred Knowledge. New York: Columbia University Press, 2016, p. 48.

a more recent study of smoking cessation after three psilocybin sessions 80% of participants were confirmed as abstinent six months later and 60% after two and one-half years, compared to typical smoking cessation therapies that have approximately 35% success rate six months post-therapy[47]. And, once again, the deeper the psilocybin-facilitated mystical state, as reflected in questionnaire scores, the higher the probability of sustained smoking abstinence. The same relation was found in alcohol addiction, supporting the view that the efficient cause of the therapeutic change is not the drug itself but the mystical state it facilitates.

These results leave no doubt as to the practical efficacy of the mystical state in engendering positive psychophysiological changes but the main issue in this chapter is whether these drug-facilitated states are similar or the same with those produced by meditation. On that point, it appears that the preponderance of evidence thus far reviewed favors the view that they are indeed the same. However, this view is not universally accepted.

It has been already mentioned that Koestler refused to accord the same status to his spontaneous mystical state in prison and to his drug-facilitated one. Others also object to equating the nature of mystical states attained in these two sets of circumstances. The most outspoken of them all appears to be the theologian and philosopher Zaehner[48]. One of the reasons for holding this position is, according to Huston Smith, the same as that of Arthur Koestler's, namely, because "his own drug experience was utterly trivial"[49] which, in view of the fact that most drug experiences are not mystical, it is not a reason at all.

But Zaehner's more substantial reason was theological. Being a Roman Catholic, he believed that the mystical state is a gift of divine grace, therefore drug-facilitated states could not be mystical, in principle. This principle may be right in some theological sense or other but it clashes with the empirical evidence. This evidence clearly suggests that mystical states are indistinguishable as described by those that experience them no matter what was the way of their attainment. And, according to the principle of the "identity of indiscernible" that seems appropriate in an empirical inquiry as this one, where the nature of data is at stake, we must conclude that the features that render experiences mystical are the same no matter how they arose.

To simply remind the reader of that fact, I will close this section with a few examples of the texture of the drug-facilitated experiences. The

47 Johnson, MW, Garcia-Romeu, A., Cosimano, MP & Griffiths, RR. Pilot study of the 5-HT2AR agonist psilocybin in the treatment of tobacco addiction. Journal of Psychopharmacology (Oxford, England), 2014, 28(11), 983–992.; Johnson, M. W., Garcia-Romeu, A., & Griffiths, RR. Long-term follow-up of psilocybin-facilitated smoking cessation. The American Journal of Drug and Alcohol Abuse, 2017, 43(1), 55–60.

48 See Zaehner, PC. Mysticism sacred and profane. New York: Oxford University Press, 1961.

49 Smith, H. Cleansing the Doors of Perception: the religious significance of entheogenic plants and chemicals. Boulder CO: Sentient Publications, 2000, p.23.

following verbatim responses of participants in one recent psilocybin study[50] are obviously similar to ejaculations of mystics throughout the ages: "Feelings of gratefulness, a great remembrance of humility....of my being in and within the infinite". Or "It changes what I believe...we are all one and divine". Or "Rich Joy and Awe. My body melting and becoming one with Universe". Or "there is a meaningful presence that humbles any human heart".

I doubt that anyone would claim that the above sentences could not be descriptions of a state attained through prayer or meditation any more than this response of a participant in another psilocybin experiment: "I was humbled and honored to be in this presence. This presence was a feeling, not something I saw or heard. I only felt it, but it felt more real than any reality I have experienced. And it was a familiar place too. One I had felt before. It was when I surrendered to this, that I felt like I let go. I was gone... or I should say this earthly part of me was. I was still on the couch in some sort of suspended animation awaiting my return. I was in the void. This void had a strange and indescribable quality to it in that there was nothing to it but this feeling of unconditional and undying Love. It felt like my soul was basking in the feeling of this space. I have no idea how long this lasted. Time and space did not exist there ... it was all different manifestations of this Love feeling I found myself wrapped in". p.398[51].

Finally, this description of an LSD-facilitated mystical state, narrated by Walter Pahnke, the author of the Good Friday study, who in fact experienced it, is more than simply reminiscent of similar descriptions of the Athonite Mystics' tales of the "Uncreated Light": "The most impressive and intense part of this experience was the *white light* of absolute purity and cleanness. It was like a glowing and sparkling flame of incandescent whiteness and beauty, but not really a flame—more like a gleaming white hot ingot, yet much bigger and vaster than a mere ingot. The associated feelings were those of absolute *awe, reverence and sacredness*...The white light experience was of *supreme importance*—absolutely self-validating and something worth staking your life on and put your trust in. The white light itself was so penetrating and intense that it was not possible to look directly at it. It was not in the room with me, but we were both somewhere else—and my body was left far behind" p. 74. (Emphases in the original)[52].

50 Garcia-Romeu, A, Griffiths, RR. and Johnson, MW. Psilocybin-occasioned mystical experiences in the treatment of tobacco addiction. Current Drug Abuse Reviews. 2014, 7(3), 157–164. (From Table 2).

51 Barrett, FS and Griffiths, RR. Classic hallucinogens and mystical experiences: Phenomenology and neural correlates. Current Topics in Behavioral Neurosciences. 2018, 36: 393–430.

52 Richards, WA. Sacred Knowledge. New York: Columbia University Press, 2016.

4 Questioning the Reliability of Mystical States

Identifying Features

Identifying the Reliable Features of the Mystical State

No two mystical experiences are ever alike. Not all mystics call their experience an encounter with the Uncreated Light, for example, although they all express one way or the other the radical transmutation of their inner vision. Not every mystic feels overflowing with love and compassion but all are overwhelmed by something positive that may be called bliss or serenity as well as love. More to the point, not all mystics express the ineffable with the same words but with those that in their (conventional) experience best approximate it. The same is true for the commentators, whether they are also mystics or not. And, since conventional experiences and the conventional ways of verbalizing them vary across individuals and cultures, the descriptions of the ineffable state are bound to vary commensurably.

No wonder then that the reader approaching the literature of mysticism, must wade through a tangle of suggestive yet not always apt or unambiguous descriptions like the one below, taken from a recent summary of opinions of various commentators regarding the nature of the mystical state[1]: 'cosmic wholeness'; 'an integrative recovery of pre-existing universal consciousness'; 'apprehension of the mind of God in nature; apprehension of God in nature'; 'a priori knowledge of the One in and behind phenomena'; 'identity with the pure consciousness or 'self' beyond nature'; 'a paradoxical identity-in-difference of sensory phenomena'; 'extension of pure consciousness into nature'; 'mania brought on by mental illness or other causes'; 'nostalgia for intra-uterine absorption'; 'unity with an inner, mental model of the world'; 'persistence of inclusive, infantile ideation in the adult mind'; 'individuation through a return to the unconscious'; 'a reparative psychological response to childhood loss'; 'emotional investment following temporal-lobe seizure'; 'microseizures in the temporal lobes'; 'changes to the neurophysiological substrates of the self';

1 In Marshall, P. Mystical Encounters with the Mystical World, New York. Oxford University Press, 2005 pp. 6–8 and 10–11.

'input changes to the parietal lobes'; 'consciousness expansion through influx of the subliminal' and 'contact with mind intrinsic to the world at large'.

The tangle becomes denser when we consider the following list of features that according to different commentators define the extrovertive, in this case, mystical state: *Unity* or feeling part of the whole; the world contained within; everything intimately connected; (a sense of) community; *Self* or relaxation of individual identity; identification with persons, animals, plants, objects, even the entire cosmos; discovery of deeper self. *Knowledge* i.e., intuitive, all-encompassing knowledge, a sense of "knowing everything"; specific questions (are) answered instantaneously; insights into order, harmony, and perfection of the world, the meaning of suffering, evolutionary development, the rightness of things; "all shall be well"; recognition that one has "come home". *Love:* All-embracing love; a sense of being deeply loved. *Beauty*: Extraordinary beauty; everything equally beautiful. *Miscellaneous feelings*: Bliss, joy, elation, uplift, peace, relief, gratitude, wonder, power, fearlessness, humor, surprise, insignificance, humility, unworthiness, awe, terror, discomfort with sheer intensity. *Time:* Time "stops"; past, present, future coexist; harmonious flow. *Reality:* Sense of contact with normally hidden depths of reality. *Realness:* "Very real"—ordinary experience seems less real. *Life:* Everything animated with "life", "consciousness", "energy"; things once thought living are lifeless in comparison. *Presence:* A (sense of) 'presence' or 'power' in nature or in the immediate vicinity. *Attention:* Heightened awareness; focused attention; clarity. *Vision:* (A) special light suffuses or obliterates surroundings; vivid colors; transparency; vision of cosmic scope. *Sound:* Silence; "music". *Body:* Sensations (felt) through the body or at places along the spine. *Fusion*: Light, love, bliss, knowledge fused together; synaesthetic fusion of sensory contents Paranormal: Extrasensory perceptions; out-of-the-body experience" pp. 27–28 (parentheses mine)[2]. To address the question of validity of such pronouncements is impossible until their referent, whether it be the experience itself or its referent and, before that, their reliability, is established.

The different predicates that have been ascribed to the mystical state fall into two classes. The first consists of predicates that do not repeat with any regularity. Most of them are readily recognized as interpretations and opinions about the (always hypothetical) causes of the mystical state or its function and significance but not its aspects qua mystical state. Good examples of such are the expressions quoted before "nostalgia for intrauterine absorption" or "individuation through a return to the unconscious".

The second class consists of predicates that do recur reliably in the testimonies of the mystics and are readily recognizable as attributes or features of the mystical experience itself or of its referent (or content or object).

2 Ibid.

These may also be further divided into two sets. I will be referring to the one as the set of genuine or core features, such as the feature "awe", because they appear in practically every description of the mystical state independently of the cultural background of the mystics. To the second I will be referring as the set of culturally conditioned features, an example of which could be "God's energy" or "Divinity" because they only occur in the testimonies of mystics of a specific theological and cultural background.

I have gone about the task of assigning features to the two sets by following on the steps of commentators who have extracted such features from original reports of mystical experiences in the past, in addition to applying my own judgment after studying those reports to which I have had direct or indirect access. The procedure has never been strictly objective because not all mystics have the story-telling power of a Huxley or a Koestler and not all have unerring memories. Nor do all commentators interpret the verbalizations of the mystics in the same way. This is especially true for original testimonies expressed in unfamiliar linguistic idioms of bygone eras that are available only in translation. Nevertheless, the consistency with which some features recur in all testimonies and the consistency among the renderings of them by the commentators vouch, in my opinion, for their reliability. As for what is meant here by consistency, can be glimpsed by comparing the several extensive quotations of mystics' testimonies spread throughout the previous chapters for the purpose of illustrating (though not demonstrating) precisely this point. In the following paragraphs and in the next two sections I will be discussing the first set of the genuine features exclusively and I will briefly comment on the second set of culturally conditioned ones in the last section of this chapter.

The first, in the modern literature of the West, to derive an unambiguous set of core features that characterize both, the introvertive and extrovertive mystical states was William James. In his opinion, the following list represents what is common to all authentic mystical experience: "*Ineffability*: The handiest of the marks" he tells us "by which I classify a state of mind as mystical is negative. The subject of it immediately says that it defies expression that no adequate report of its contents can be given in words. *Noetic Quality*: Although so similar to states of feeling, mystical states seem to those who experience them to be also states of knowledge. They are states of insight into depths of truth unplumbed by the discursive intellect. They are illuminations, revelations, full of significance and importance, all inarticulate though they remain; and as a rule, they carry with them a curious sense of authority for after time. *Transiency*: Mystical states cannot be sustained for long. *Passivity:* Although the oncoming of mystical states may be facilitated by preliminary voluntary operations, as by fixing the attention, or going through certain bodily performances, or in other ways which manuals of mysticism prescribe; yet when the characteristic sort of consciousness once has set in, the mystic feels as if his own will were in abeyance, and indeed sometimes as if he were grasped and held by a superior power"[3].

A similar list of genuine features is provided by Professor Suzuki, who introduced Zen Buddhism in the West. His list includes:

"*Irrationality*. By this I mean that satori is not a conclusion to be reached by reasoning, and defies all intellectual determination. Those who have experienced it are always at a loss to explain it coherently or logically. *Intuitive Insight*. That there is noetic quality in mystic experiences has been pointed out by (William) James...Another name for satori is "kensho" (chien-hsing in Chinese) meaning "to see essence or nature", which apparently proves that there is "seeing" or "perceiving" in satori...Without this noetic quality satori will lose all its pungency, for it is really the reason of satori itself. *Authoritativeness*. By this I mean that the knowledge realized by satori is final, that no amount of logical argument can refute it. Being direct and personal it is sufficient unto itself. All that logic can do here is to explain it, to interpret it in connection to other kinds of knowledge with which our minds are filled. Satori is thus a form of perception, an inner perception, which takes place in the most interior part of consciousness. *Affirmation*. What is authoritative and final can never be negative. Though the satori experience is sometimes expressed in negative terms, it is essentially an affirmative attitude towards all things that exist; it accepts them as they come along regardless of their moral values. *Sense of the Beyond*. ...in satori there is always what we may call a sense of the Beyond; the experience indeed is my own but I feel it to be rooted elsewhere. The individual shell in which my personality is so solidly encased explodes at the moment of satori. Not, necessarily, that I get unified with a being greater than myself or absorbed in it, but that my individuality, which I found rigidly held together and definitely kept separate from other individual existences, becomes loosened somehow from its tightening grip and melts away into something indescribable, something which is of quite a different order from what I am accustomed to. The feeling that follows is that of complete release or a complete rest—the feeling that one has arrived finally at the destination...As far as the psychology of satori is considered, a sense of the Beyond is all we can say about it; to call this the Beyond, the Absolute, or God, or a Person is to go further than the experience itself and to plunge into a theology or metaphysics. *Impersonal Tone*. Perhaps the most remarkable aspect of the

3 James, W. Varieties of Religious Experiences. New York: Longmans, Green and Co. 1902/1917 p.p. 370–371.

Zen experience is that it has no personal note in it as is observable in Christian mystic experiences. *Feeling of exaltation.* That this feeling inevitably accompanies satori is due to the fact that it is the breaking-up of the restriction imposed on one as an individual being, and this breaking up is not a mere negative incident but quite a positive one fraught with signification because it means an infinite expansion of the individual. *Momentariness.* Satori comes upon one abruptly and is a momentary experience. In fact, if it is not abrupt and momentary, it is not satori[4].

It is clear that there is an obvious overlap in the features these two commentators have extracted from the testimonies of mystics they have studied, although the overlap is sometimes obscured by differences in expression employed by them. As previously mentioned, contemporary questionnaires and scales employed in researching the nature of the mystical states, especially those that are drug-facilitated, have been based on the list of features Walter Stace derived from his study of extrovertive and introvertive experiences of mystics of many cultures which also overlap with those of James and of Suzuki. His list includes: *The Unifying Vision*: all things are One. The more concrete apprehension of the One as an *inner subjectivity, or Life*, in all things. The *Nonspatial, nontemporal* nature of the One. A *Sense of objectivity or reality*: the One exists objectively. A "feeling" of *Blessedness, peace*, etc. A Feeling *of the holy, sacred, or divine.* A sense of *Paradoxicality. Ineffability*: the mystics claim that the experience cannot be described accurately with words[5].

In the Good Friday experiment, the questionnaire Walter Pahnke employed includes items corresponding to each of the features in Stace's list: "*Unity*: a sense of cosmic oneness. *Transcendence of Time and Space.* Deeply Felt *Positive Mood. Sense of Sacredness. Noetic Quality*: a feeling of *insight or illumination. Paradocicality*: A person may realize that he/she is experiencing, for example, "an identity of opposites", yet it seems to make sense at the time. *Alleged ineffability. Transiency:* the experience passes. *Persisting Positive Changes* in Attitudes and Behavior"[6].

The original Mystical Experience Questionnaire, developed by Pahnke has in recent years been studied extensively, has been validated in several

4 Suzuki, DT. Zen Buddhism: Selected Writings of D.T, Suzuki. New York: Anchor Books, 1956), pp. 103–108.

5 Stace, WT. Mysticism and Philosophy. Los Angeles: Jeremy P Tarcher, Inc., 1960. pp. 131–132.

6 See e.g. Pahnke, W. The Psychedelic Mystical Experience in the Human Encounter With Death, Psychedelic Review, 1971, Number 11,

studies, and has also been factor-analyzed[7]. On the basis of that analysis, it is suggested that the mystical experience can be reduced to four factors. The first includes the features of "unity", "noetic quality" and "sacredness"; the second the feature of "positive mood"; the third the "transcendence of time and space" and the fourth the feature of "ineffability".

For the purpose of detecting the presence of mystical states and their long-term effects on the behavior and mentation of the mystics in their conventional life, this psychometric instrument has been found to be very useful. It has also been found to be useful in that, in connection with the overlapping qualitative descriptions of the mystical state by the various commentators, establishes the set of features that define most, if not all, mystical states. The significance of the set of the culturally conditioned features that are not included in this scale will be commented on, as mentioned, in the last section of this chapter.

Classification of the Genuine Features of the Mystical State

To properly address the validity of the culture-independent, core features that define the mystical state they must be further divided according to whether they can be said to refer to the experience itself or to its object and that object's attributes. This separation is necessary because the validity of the features defining the object of the experience refers to the ontological status of that object. That is to say, whether the object (including its defining attributes) exists independently of the subject that experiences it or knows it, whereas the validity of features of the experience itself (such as its transiency, its ineffability or its affective coloring is judged on a different basis as is detailed in the final chapter of this book.

But to separate the features of the experience itself from those that belong to and define the object of the experience is a treacherous exercise. Even more treacherous is the extraction of the common meaning of various synonymous or near-synonymous expressions and give it a name that is proper for it. Therefore, I can only hope that the reader will soon appreciate that I have been very careful not to misinterpret the expressions of the mystics and the commentators while engaging in this necessary procedure of feature extraction and naming on their basis.

Features Attributable to the Experience Itself

To begin with, the mystical experience is knowledge or awareness of something. On this point, there is no disagreement whatsoever among the

7 See e.g. Maclean, KA., Leoutsakos, JM., Johnson, MW., & Griffiths, RR. Factor analysis of the mystical experience questionnaire: A study of experiences occasioned by the hallucinogen psilocybin. Journal for the Scientific Study of Religion. 2012, 51(4), 721–737.

mystics and the commentators ancient or contemporary. This is the meaning of James' expression "noetic quality" and Suzuki's "intuitive insight". It is, as certainly, not awareness of sensations or of percepts or of any familiar concepts. It is, in fact, "ineffable" as all mystics and commentators agree. And, when the mystics attempt to rationalize and articulate its object, the resulting transposition of that ineffable object into familiar semantic categories renders it "paradoxical". For example, the object of knowledge becomes absolute emptiness, darkness or silence—the Void of the Buddhist mystics—but also the fountain of all that exists, the Plenum whence all things proceed, the Divine light, the all-inclusive One of Plotinus etc.

Mystical knowledge is also definitively "authoritative", incontestable. There is absolute and unconditional certainty on the part of the mystic that whatever exactly its referent may be, the knowledge of it is true and infallible and its referent is more "real" than any object among those that constitute our conventional reality. Then, this noetic illumination is "transient". Typically it lasts anywhere from minutes to hours of conventional clock time and typically has a sudden onset; it exhibits "instantaneity". Finally, the experience is characterized by what James called "passivity", a form of abdication of the personal will, expressed as lack of concern for whatever may happen and perhaps as fearlessness—a feature that will be discussed below along with other features that may refer either to the experience itself or its referent. The same "passivity" is clearly implied in all expressions conveying the notion that the self of the mystic is abolished or that it melts into the universal Self or the "One" and disappears therein.

These are, then, the genuine, or core features that are universally recognized as defining an experience as mystical, but they are not all. Another core feature of the mystical state—the cardinal one according to Stace[8]—is the absolute merging or the union of the personal self of the experiencing subject, the *Atman* of Hinduism, with the *Brahman*, the universal Self, or the universal Spirit or Consciousness. But the testimony of the mystics and the opinions of commentators vary widely as to the meaning of this "merging" or "union". The meaning, in fact, varies from a relation of "beholding" or of "encountering" and "viewing" the object of the experience to a total merging of the personal consciousness and becoming identical with it thus creating a perfectly undifferentiated unity—the unity Stace considers the single most important defining feature of any genuine mystical state.

Moreover the meaning varies in that the union may be viewed as being consummated only during the mystical state or viewed as a perennial and eternal reality that the mystical state simply reveals. The meaning of the union varies further with its many different possible forms: Union may be a form of "contact" of the mystic's mind with the Mind intrinsic

8 Stace, WT. The Teachings of the Mystics. New York: Mentor Books, 1960; Stace, WT. Mysticism and Philosophy. Los Angeles: Jeremy P Tarcher, Inc., 1960).

in the world at large; or it may be the feeling that one becomes part of the world in a way different from the conventional one; or of being identified with parts of the world and similar such relations that Paul Marshall[9] has classified into seven kinds: "Integral unity"—the apprehension of all things as a seamless whole; "immersive unity", where the subject feels immersed into the whole like Koestler's drop of water becoming part of the ocean; "identificatory unity" where the self is identified with the whole universe; "incorporative unity" in which the world becomes engulfed by or enfolded into the self of the experiencing subject; "communal unity" or the sense of connection through empathy or love with other people; "inter-connective unity" where the mystic realizes the existence of specific links among objects; "source unity" corresponding to extrovertive unity and other species of merging and unification such as "unity-in-difference" which is a sub-species of "unity-in-duality" and "unity-in-multiplicity".

Needless to say, how common among mystics is each of these kinds of unification, is as obscure as any other mode of merging mentioned. But of much more fundamental importance is another ambiguity regarding the meaning of the merging or of the union of the personal self and the universal Self that was mentioned in passing above but merits further elaboration: One possibility is that the mystical knowing is becoming aware of the union of two things that exist separately from one another, the personal mind or self and the universal mind of Self, whereby the self becomes either a part of the Self or identical with the Self, *while the mystical state lasts.* A second possibility is that the self and the Self are always and will always remain either identical or the self is always and will always remain part of the Self, in which case the mystical knowledge is simply the *transient awareness of this eternal fact.* Although Stace[10] appears to favor the latter interpretation, where the self is always identical with the Self, the former possibility cannot, in fairness, be excluded.

To summarize, the genuine experience-specific features apposed above are: *knowledge, ineffable* and *certain*; *transiency; passivity* and a sense of *contact or interaction* with the referent of the experience. The precise form of this interaction, on the other hand, whether it be a union of a particular kind, consummated during the mystical state, or an eternal one but one only recognized during the state, is of no consequence for the present inquiry.

Also of no consequence are the host of other features or attributes of the mystical state that vary from mystic to mystic and from one commentator to the next such as: "heightened awareness"; "discovery of deeper self"; "insight into order and harmony"; "relaxation of personal boundaries"; "expansion of consciousness through influx of the subliminal"; "nostalgia

9 Marshall, P. Mystical Encounters with the Mystical World, New York. Oxford University Press, 2005.

10 Stace, WT. Mysticism and Philosophy. Los Angeles: Jeremy P Tarcher, Inc., 1960.

for intrauterine absorption"; "infantile ideation"; "individuation via return to the unconscious"; "mania"; "response to seizures"; "response to parietal lobe discharges"; and other such psychological and neurophysiological attributes mentioned earlier many of which qualify less as features of the experience itself and more as hypothetical causes of it. And, they are of no consequence, because regardless of whether they are culturally conditioned attributes of the state or idiosyncratic opinions of each mystic or commentator, they are unrelated to the nature of the genuine state the validity of which is the sole focus of this inquiry.

Features Attributable to the Object of the Experience

Separating features of the experience *qua experience* from those that may be attributable to its object is, as I commented earlier, a treacherous exercise. Yet, there is no doubt that Stace's opinion that mystical experience is awareness of an already existing unity of the mystic's mind with the universal Mind notwithstanding, mystics do "know" or at least they report consistently that the object of their knowledge is something beyond themselves; therefore it is something with which they may or may not be identical or something of which they may or may not come to be a part. To be sure, in some cases we do have testimony justifying Stace's opinion but, as it has been documented previously and will be discussed again, in most cases the mystics' knowledge (and most certainly their testimony) is of something beyond themselves, with which they may unite or interact: "In satori", Suzuki tells us, again, "there is always what we may call a sense of the Beyond; the experience is indeed my own but I feel it to be rooted elsewhere". Therefore, at this point the only thing we can assert with reasonable certainty on this question is that there is such a thing as the "object" of the experience and leave it at that. We can also assert with considerable certainty that one of the central and at the same time most inexpressible feature of mystical object is its *luminosity*.

This feature, though its name suggests a perceptual origin is entirely noetic. It is known with certainty although it is not conventionally conceptual. Its source is no more outside the mystic than inside him. Yet it is an attribute of the encountered object: some times you go towards and inside it and other times it overwhelms and engulfs you. But this uncreated light is not even light; it is as much light as it is total darkness but an utterly brilliant and luminous darkness. What exactly the mystics struggle to express with this attribute of their encounter cannot be but a matter of speculation. However, there are two things one may assert with reasonable certainty: first, that it must be something that strikes all mystics in a similar way about the mystical object, for otherwise there would likely be considerably more variability in their verbal attempts to describe it. And, second, that it is an attribute of the object and not of those that behold and know it.

But the mystical object has additional specific features as well. One such feature is the object's organic wholeness or unity. By that is meant something more akin to a chemical compound where the individuality of the constituent elements is adjusted so as not to compromise its essential nature as a unity, and something definitely opposite to a mixture or a mosaic of constituent elements externally conjoined and externally interacting with each other. Second, the object's nature is reported as akin to mind or to consciousness, albeit not necessarily to a personal consciousness (the Zen mystics, unlike the Christian of Muslim mystics "know" it to be impersonal) and less akin to any known form of matter and energy, in that it is "known" to lie beyond time and space.

These are then the only genuine features of the mystical "object" that are universally shared: the object of mystical knowledge is a *luminous* one; it forms an *organic whole,* is *consciousness-like* or *mind-like* and *eternal* (beyond space and time). These, at any rate, were the only features that could be extracted with reasonable certainty as the common meaning of the following array of features attributed to it by mystics and commentators: True reality; Divinity; God; uncreated light; the Godhead; God's abode; Universal Self; Presence; cosmic wholeness; cosmic consciousness; something impersonal; void; plenum; pure consciousness; Brahman; One; mind of God; mind in Nature; something energetic; something alive; the Creation and the Creator combined; only the Creation; only the Creator; the Creator's essence; the Creator's energy.

It is obvious that these expressions owe to a great extent their specificity to different theological or metaphysical credos and are clearly conditioned by them. Because of that, it is often the case that the adherents of a particular theological dogma, let us say of a theistic religion, would claim that the only authentic mystical state is one where the mystic's soul communes with the energy but not the essence of God—an issue on which I have commented earlier—whereas all other testimonies of mystical experiences are somehow inauthentic. But no authenticity of any state can be possibly established on the basis of contradictory or even merely discordant attributes.

Features that May be Attributed Either to the Experience qua Experience or to its Object

The referent of mystical knowledge is variously said to be good, beautiful, loving awesome, holy and sacred. But it is also said, and with the same frequency, that the experience itself is beautiful, good, filled with a sense of love, of awe, sacredness etc. Now it is a philosophical riddle of long-standing as to whether attributes like "beauty" and the rest of them are purely subjective feelings or attributes of the referent that inspires them. "Beauty is in the eye of the beholder" is an old maxim also expressed in the subtler language of philosophy by

Santayana[11] as "objectified pleasure"; subjective pleasure, that is, which is unconsciously projected onto the external object that inspires it. Only, neither the popular maxim nor the philosopher's dictum solves the problem because the beautiful object must possess itself some characteristic that triggers pleasure in the subject in contrast to other, not beautiful objects, that fail to do so. But, this being not a philosophical disquisition into the nature of aesthetic or value judgments, we have to leave things as they appear: ambiguous. Beauty, goodness, love, awe, holiness, sacredness, terror, joy, bliss, elation, uplift, peace, relief, gratitude, wonder, power, humor, surprise, humility, intensity, discomfort, rest, release, exaltation, infinite expansiveness and blessedness, among other such features that are variously said to emerge during mystical states, may be safely said to reduce, except for terror, to one invariant feature: an over-all positive affective glow and one that has positive long-term repercussions in the mystic's life.

I said "affective glow" to convey the fact that even the affective features of the mystical state are *noetic* in nature and have very little, if anything, in common with ordinary pleasures and ordinary pains and terrors. Terror, fear, stress of discomfort in general is clearly not among the positive affects, noetic or otherwise. And, although it is not met with, in most mystical states, it appears frequently enough to deserve consideration. It used to be much more common in the past in cases where the set and the setting, that is, the personality of the mystic and the context of the mystical experience were not carefully considered. It is less frequent now, especially in drug-facilitated states attained in the context of controlled clinical studies. Nevertheless, it persists.

Clearly, though, it is not among the genuine features of the mystical state because it is not reported as part of most of them unless the words "fear" or "terror" is used by mystics to express the species of sentiment that is also called "awe". Now, awe, is a genuine feature of the mystical state even if it is also felt during the visions that sometimes "bracket" the mystical experience.

There is, however, yet another "affective" feature that is worth mentioning in that it marks all authentic mystical experiences: the feature of fearlessness or lack of concern. It is not clear if that feature is related to the "passivity" characteristic of the entire state, that was commented earlier, or to a tacit trust in the benevolence of the object of mystical knowledge that has filled the vacuum, the personal will creates with its absence, which absence marks all authentic mystical states.

Not being able to conclude with any certainty if the features under consideration are attributes of the experience itself or attributes of its object, and to avoid the error of endowing the mystical object with attributes it may not possess, we will consider them all features of the experience itself.

11 Santayana, G. The Sense of Beauty. New York: Barns and Noble Publishing, Inc. 1896/2005.

Therefore it appears that three basic features can be added to the set of genuine ones characterizing the experience itself: *positive affective coloring, awe* and *fearlessness or unconcern* whereas the specific affective features such as love, serenity and bliss appear to be culture-specific. For example, judging from the frequency of occurrence, it seems that serenity is mentioned more by Buddhist and Zen mystics and love by Christians.

Could the Reliably Reported Features be Fabrications?

Reliable reports, however, as well as reliably reported core features could sometimes be fraudulent. Yet, as it happens, there is no reason to consider the testimonies of the mystics and the pronouncements of commentators as fabrications: Fabrication can either be coordinated, such that all or most mystics and commentators conspire to describe consistently a particular kind of state with the same set of features, or it can be random or circumstantial. To propose coordinated fraud that includes ancient Hindu monks, saints of medieval Christianity and volunteers in formal experiments conducted in universities today, strains credulity, to say the least.

It is true that those who have experienced the mystical knowledge are philosophers, saints of different religions, intellectuals, and also people who happened to be visited by the experience unaccountably as well as people who ingested psychedelics for entertainment and were stunned to find themselves transported into the mystical realm. But it is also true that most of those who sought the experience deliberately belong to that perennial fraternity of the seekers of the "hidden reality". And, that fact raises the possibility that the reports of the discovery of that hidden world may have been deliberately distorted so as to fulfill the mystics' ambitions and justify their expectations.

There are, however, several reasons that militate against that possibility: First, some mystics persist in their belief that they have acquired true knowledge about the essence of all that exists even at the cost of their life. A good example of this is provided by the already mentioned case of the Sufi mystic Al Hallaj who claimed that his sacred mystical knowledge was about the undifferentiated unity of his own self with God and was crucified in Baghdad in 922 by his fellow theologians for not renouncing his "blasphemous" conviction that he was, in essence, God[12]. Second, the consistency of the reports regarding the nature of the experience would have required a vast conspiracy spanning all continents and extending over centuries and hundreds of cultures. But, as already mentioned, no such arrangement is realistically feasible. Third, some of the witnesses of the sacred revelation have come upon it unexpectedly, without seeking it and

12 Stace, WT. The Teachings of the Mystics. New York: Mentor Books, 1960., p.p. 201–202}.

without harboring any notions as to what it would be like. I am referring here to those who had "spontaneous" illuminations, especially at a very young age, and those that came upon the experience by accident, while pursuing a different form of drug-facilitated entertainment.

One may go on adducing reasons that render the hypothesis of fraudulent witnesses unrealistic but the three just mentioned ought to suffice in showing that it is baseless. Of course, there remains the possibility that the reports of the mystics were not and are not deliberately distorted but distorted nevertheless, albeit unintentionally; that the mystical knowledge is simply the fulfillment of expectations or the objectification of a desperate wish on the part of the zealots to experience the sacred hidden reality. This hypothesis though, does not account, once again, for the reports of thrill seekers that have had no such wishes and expectations. But the hypothesis ought to be and will be assessed in the next section of this chapter not only because it is possible that the "thrill seekers" may have had advanced knowledge of the nature of the experience they may encounter, but because of the possibility that the mystical experience is (for reasons to be discussed soon) an entirely subjective construction and has no objective value whatsoever.

Random fabrications, on the other hand, would produce random descriptions—not the same ones of most mystical states. Moreover, there are no obvious incentives for the mystics to fabricate, either systematically or randomly, extraordinary and incomprehensible experiences, requiring at times the expenditure of tremendous pains and efforts, unless they intended to attract attention and status. But rarely, if ever, mystics enjoyed special status for being mystics and most of them, especially in the past, avoided relating publicly their experiences because, whether true or fabricated, they would most likely invite suspicion, incomprehension and ostracism. In fact, throughout history, mystics have been reluctant to publicize their experiences and at times expressly advised not to communicate them to people outside their intimate circle of initiates.

The Status of the Culturally Conditioned and the Genuine Features

The notion that many of the mystical features reflect cultural influences, therefore they are subjective constructions of dubious ontological status is true. I have already commented on the obvious fact that many features do reflect the religious beliefs of the mystics. But these are not genuine features of the mystical state because they do not co-define all mystical states but are the readily recognizable accretions to it representing not the experience itself or its referent but the conventional beliefs that color the mystic's interpretation of that experience. And the proof of that is that they vary reliably from the one cultural context to the next[13].

Consider for instance the conflicting interpretations as to what exactly is the nature of the object of the experience: is it the Creation and the Creator combined; or is it only the Creation or only the Creator; or is it the Creator's abode but not His essence? Which one — if anyone— of the many such claims is valid is impossible to establish, since no other indications exist beyond the conflicting interpretations of the experience offered by mystics of different cultures and the obviously culturally conditioned ones offered by mystics sharing the same religious beliefs. Similarly impossible, and for the same reason, is the assessment of the validity of alternative interpretations of the nature of "merging" or of the union of the subject with the object of the mystical experience. It cannot be true that the union is both eternal and transient. Nor can it be true at the same time that the mystical union is both a "vision" of the One and the "undifferentiated unification" of the self with it. It seems, therefore, that the closest we can come to an evaluation for those of the culturally conditioned features that are mutually exclusive is to say that *either one or none of them is true*. And we will never know which one of them—if any, is the correct one.

Having separated the genuine features of the mystical state from all the rest we can now concentrate on them alone. The one set of them defines the experience itself while the other set defines its object. Those that define the experience itself are, once more, the following: The mystical state is *knowledge* of something real that is independent of or beyond the experiencing subject; it is absolutely *incontestable* knowledge; it is *ineffable*, and *paradoxical* when mediated and expressed in terms of familiar concepts and words; it entails a form of *passivity* marked by the absence of will to do anything and the certainty of an *intimate contact* or interaction between its "object" and the knowing self. It is *affectively positive* and it is marked by *awe* but also *fearlessness* or *unconcern*. Finally, though *transient* it is remembered and has palpable repercussions in the life of the mystic. On the other hand, the genuine features of the object of the mystical knowledge are its *luminosity*, the *organic unity* of all its parts or aspects, its being *akin to mind or consciousness* rather than to matter or energy as the latter are commonly defined, and its being *eternal* or beyond space and time.

The validity of these two sets of genuine features can now be evaluated. However, the two sets are not valid in the same way. The validity of those

13 William J Wainwright, in his insightful book on Mysticism (Sussex: the Harvester Press, 1981, p.p. 107–110) in countering the arguments of the constructivists who claim that all mystical objects are culturally-conditioned constructions, therefore false, argues that the fact that some mystics identify the object of mystical knowledge as Jesus and others as some Indian divinity (i.e. the fact that they are partly culturally-conditioned) does not render them false or delusional. I would agree that they are not *necessarily* false. However, because they *may be* false, I have adopted the strictest criterion and I have excluded them altogether from the set of genuine features.

that define the object of knowledge consists in the object's existing independently of the subjects that experience it; that it is *not* a construction of the subjects' mind without a referent outside that mind; that it is not a delusion or a pseudo-hallucination.

On the other hand, the validity of those features that are attributed to the experience itself can either be judged on the basis of the subject's authority that claims them to be true or on the basis of the pragmatic criterion that James,[14] among others, has proposed, namely whether they have important and lasting repercussions on the mystics' conventional life that follows the mystical illumination.

It is mandatory that the validity of both sets of genuine features be challenged because the possibilities of error are many and varied. The study of perception has made us aware of the fact that illusions have the uncanny power of masquerading as true percepts even when one knows that they are not veridical: One may know, on the basis of all sorts of independent determinations that what is perceived as converging railroad tracks in the distance are, in fact, parallel; one may know that the image of water on the road ahead is not actually water but a mirage, yet one and all cannot escape the illusions because we all share the same perceptual and cognitive apparatus with its limitations and peculiarities.

The study of psychopathology has also made us aware of how delusions and true hallucinations due to abnormal changes in brain activity may appear incontestably true to those that experience them. And, there is no doubt that each and every veridical and false percept and each and every true as well as false notion corresponds to (and possibly depends on) a particular and distinct brain state, which in turn depends on the brain's chemistry, raising the possibility that all experience is epiphenomenal, that is, fake or causally inert. Moreover, psychological and philosophical analysis has shown that percepts are to a large extent subjective constructions and not mere passive records of external events; constructions that depend on the milieu in which one grows up, especially the cultural milieu and all the tacit beliefs and attitudes that this milieu entails. Finally, that they also depend far less on the nature of the external objects than passive records do. Perhaps most importantly, philosophical scholarship has shown us how much more of what we believe is conditioned by the kind of world legend—that amalgam of metaphysical and moral assumptions discussed in the third section of the second chapter—which we inadvertently carry with us, than by the evidence of each case. With all these caveats in mind, we may now proceed to examine the validity of mystical experiences keeping at bay, to the degree possible, all sources of error and all preconceived biases.

14 James, W. On Pragmatism. In William James Writings 1902-1910. Library of America. Literary Classics of the United States, Inc., 1987.

5 Questioning the Validity of Mystical States

Opinions and Objections

The Range of Opinions on the Validity of the Mystics' Claims

As it has been emphasized repeatedly, mystics do assert that their mystical experiences are valid and there is evidence that this conviction stays with most of them years after their illumination. Among the non-mystics, most ardent adherents to the perennial world legend also consider the testimony of the mystics valid since it supplies corroborating evidence for their own beliefs. For the same reason, the adherents to the Democritean world view consider the mystical state a delusion. But, whereas the conviction of the mystics may constitute evidence for the validity of their mystical knowledge without further justification (see next section), the opinion of the uninitiated either for or against the validity of this knowledge does require justification if it is to be more than an unreasoned, therefore unreasonable, acceptance of what is merely dictated by one's metaphysical bias. Accordingly, in the sections that follow, such justifications for both types of opinions will be presented and discussed.

Of the many commentators some believe that the validity of the mystical states is indeterminate. This opinion will be discussed extensively in the next section. Others accept the validity of only some of the mystical states but not of others. A case in point here is the philosopher Zaehner[1], who argued that valid are only those mystical states that are attained through meditation and prayer to the God of monotheism, of Christianity in particular, whereas those attained with the aid of drugs are not. This opinion has been rejected as non-valid for several reasons.[2] It should also be rejected as non-valid because it does not concern the genuine features of the mystical state but only the culturally—conditioned ones that for reasons discussed in the previous chapter do not belong to the mystical state.

1 Zaehner, PC. Mysticism Sacred and Profane. New York: Oxford University Press, 1961.

2 See e.g. Smith, H. Cleansing the Doors of Perception: the religious significance of entheogenic plants and chemicals. Boulder CO: Sentient Publications, 2000.

Other commentators accept the validity of the mystical experience without reservations especially when they happen to be mystics themselves such as Dr. Bucke, the author of "Cosmic Consciousness"[3], while others deny it. The rationale for such denials will be presented and evaluated below, in chapter 5. At present, I will discuss the uncritical acceptance of the validity of the mystical state.

I will begin with a brief description of a rather strange position that views mystical experiences as outputs of a brain mechanism evolved for the express purpose of "enabling humans to know God"[4]. This opinion is strange because it does not explain what survival advantage this mechanism conferred on the species while it was gradually evolving, that is to say, *before humans could know God through it*. Moreover, the opinion does not have probative value because it simply assumes that the object of the experience is God who exists independently of the knowing humans that He endowed them, through evolution, with the requisite brain mechanism that would enable them to come to know Him directly!

The same gratuitous settlement of the issue of the validity of the mystical states is found in the account of their "evolution", of the author of "Cosmic Consciousness", Dr. Bucke, mentioned several times in the course of this work: "...the birth of cosmic consciousness in the individual", he wrote, "is very similar to that of the birth of self-consciousness. The mind becomes overcrowded (as it were) with concepts and these are constantly becoming larger, more numerous and more and more complex; someday (the conditions being all favorable) the fusion, or what might be called the chemical union, of several of them and of certain moral elements takes place; the result is an intuition and the establishment of the intuitional mind, or, in other words, cosmic consciousness" p. 18[5].

And again, in a more sweeping account of the same "evolution" he writes: "As life arose in a world without life; as Simple Consciousness came into existence where before was mere vitality without perception; as Self Consciousness leaping wide winged from Simple Consciousness soared forth over land and sea, so shall the race of man which has been thus established, continuing its beginningless and endless ascent, make other steps (the next of which it is now in act of climbing) and attain to a yet higher life than any heretofore experienced or even conceived" p. 22[6].

Needless to say, this way of resolving the issue of the validity of the genuine features of the mystical state is or should be unacceptable to all who

3 Bucke, RM. Cosmic Consciousness: A Study in the Evolution of the Human Mind. New York: E.P. Dutton and Company, Inc. 1901.

4 Joseph, R. The limbic system and the soul: Evolution and the neuroanatomy of religious experience. Zygon. 2001, 36, 105–136.

5 Bucke, RM. Cosmic Consciousness: A Study in the Evolution of the Human Mind. New York: E.P. Dutton and Company, Inc. 1901.

6 Ibid.

are not willing to elevate conjectures to the status of evidence regardless of whether these conjectures accord with their metaphysical worldview or not.

For the same reason one ought to also reject the opinions of Aldus Huxley[7] and of Evelyn Underhill, another eminent authority on mysticism[8]: Both base their acceptance of the objective existence of the mystical object—be it the God of the theistic theologies or the Plotinian One—on the hypothesis that mind or consciousness is a universal entity that exists independently of the brain—which brain functions as a valve. Once again, conjectures, hypotheses and metaphysical theories, however reasonable they may sound, ought not to be taken as evidence. And, the objective existence of a universal mind or Brahma or God or One ought not to be justified by the hypothesis that there is a brain mechanism that behaves like a valve—a hypothesis neither more nor less valid, a priori, than the hypothesis that the brain is an engine that produces consciousness.

William James' position on this question is best summarized in the following three statements of his, taken from his lecture on Mysticism "(1) Mystical states, when well developed, usually are, and have the right to be, absolutely authoritative over the individuals to whom they come. (2) No authority emanates from them which should make it a duty for those who stand outside of them to accept their revelations uncritically. (3) They break down the authority of the non-mystical or rationalistic consciousness, based upon the understanding and the senses alone. They show it to be only one kind of consciousness. They open out the possibility of other orders of truth, in which, so far as anything in us vitally responds to them, we may freely continue to have faith"[9].

Therefore, though James endorses the validity of the mystical states for those who "vitally respond" to them, he refrains from also endorsing it unconditionally. But the question is whether there are reasons for endorsing it even when nothing "in us vitally responds" and urges us to accept it; whether, in other words there are reasons for which *we ought to accept it* regardless if we do or not.

Of special interest is the position of W.T. Stace on this issue[10]. He denies the objective, that is, the subject-independent, existence of the object of the mystical experience but only because he defines "objective" as that which exists in space and time, thus excluding anything that is not made of

7 Huxley, A. the Doors of Perception and Heaven and Hell. Harper Perennial modern Classics, 1954.

8 Underhill, E. Mysticism: A Study of the Nature and Development of Man's Spiritual Consciousness (1911). Twelfth edition published by E. P. Dutton in 1930. Republished by Dover Publications in 2002.

9 James, W. The varieties of religious experience: a study in human nature: being the Gifford lectures on natural religion delivered at Edinburgh in 1901–1902, pp. 380–430.

10 Stace, WT. Mysticism and Philosophy. Los Angeles: Jeremy P. Tarcher, Inc., 1960.

conventional matter or energy from the set of objectively existing things. But he also denies that mystical experiences are merely subjective, that is, idiosyncratic or variable, since they are the same for all mystics of all cultures throughout the ages. He calls them instead "transubjective" and assigns to them the same ontological status as that of mathematical objects, as the Platonic forms and other universals, the ontological status of which, however, is also debatable.

His verdict, moreover, rests on two propositions that I do not find compelling. The first is the definition of the "objective" just described, which denies a priori subject-independent existence to anything that is not material. The second is that, as a matter of empirical fact, the mind of the mystic and the universal Mind are identical. But it is debatable whether this is a fact since not all mystics testify to that effect; not all speak as Stace does, of an "undifferentiated union" where their own self, emptied of all sensations, thoughts and images, becomes aware of its being one with the universal Self.

The examples of mystics' testimonies, some of which have been presented in the previous pages, do raise serious doubts that the type of "undifferentiated union" Stace proclaims as actual, is the only kind of relation between the subject and the ineffable object of the mystical experience. And, it is, in fact, for this very reason that I have called the common element of all references to "union" in the testimonies of mystics, noncommitally, as some type of "contact" or "encounter" or "interaction" and not as "undifferentiated union".

More recently, another philosopher, William Wainwright, pronounced for the validity of at least some mystical states. In his book[11], he successfully deconstructs the contextualist claim that all mystical states are culturally conditioned therefore it is not possible to assess whether any of them reflects aspects of objective reality. Next, having set as his goal "to make a case for the uniqueness and validity of the theistic mystical consciousness" p. 233 he sides with the Oxford philosopher Zaehner and, against Stace, declares that there are at least two distinct types of mystical states, monistic and theistic with the latter being more likely valid.

I am not prepared to join him, or any other philosopher, for that matter, in a metaphysical disputation as to the number of varieties of mystical states. There may well be two or more just as he suggests. For my purposes, the fact that all mystical states share the core attributes empirically derived in the previous chapters suffices because it is the validity of those common attributes that concerns me here. Therefore I concur with his assessment that what he considers theistic experiences are valid but I do not exclude other experiences that share the same core features with them from that category. I do find, however, the rationale of his verdict, namely

11 Wainwright, WJ. Mysticism. Sussex: the Harvester Press, 1981

that "the analogy between sense experience and mystical consciousness is sufficiently close to provide a good reason for believing that mystical experiences are valid". p. 232 rather wanting.

Whether acceptable or not to the reader, these positive verdicts regarding the validity of the mystical states remain unacceptable to me because, once again, they are mainly grounded on hypotheses or conjectures and not on evidence. But not all opinions are in favor of the objective validity of the mystical state. Most, in fact, are emphatically negative. The latter come in two basic varieties: first are those that deny the possibility of assessing whether the genuine features of mystical states are true or not. Second, are those that assert that the content of mystical knowledge is definitely a delusion. Both will be discussed next.

Is the Validity of the Mystical Knowledge Indeterminate?

There is a philosophical school, the school of contextualism, which claims that it is impossible to assess the truth status of the mystical state. In the words of one of its main proponents, in one of his best-known position papers[12] we read:

"...(In this chapter) it is not being argued either that mystical experiences do not happen, or that what they claim may not be true, only that there can be no grounds for deciding this question, i.e. of showing that they are true even if they are, in fact, true. Moreover, even this disclaimer requires the further declaration that, though no philosophical argument is capable of proving the veracity of mystical experience, one would be both dogmatic and imprudent to decide a priori that mystical claims are mumbo-jumbo, especially given the wide variety of such claims by men of genius and/or intense religious sensitivity over the centuries as well as across all cultural divisions. Nor does it seem reasonable to reduce these multiple and variegated claims to mere projected 'psychological states' which are solely the product of interior states of consciousness" pp. 22–23, (parenthesis mine).

I wholeheartedly agree that the validity of any kind of experience and not only mystical, cannot be proven. Proof is only possible where propositions of formal logic and mathematics are concerned. I also agree that no philosophical—by which I understand metaphysical as opposed to empirical—argument can provide the proof. Instead, as I stated in the introductory chapter, the question of the validity of the mystical states may be decided on the basis of the preponderance of evidence. But, to return to what I assume to be the intended meaning of the contextualist thesis,

12 Katz, ST. Language, Epistemology, and Mysticism in ST Kantz Ed. Mysticism and Philosophical analysis. New York: Oxford University Press, 1978.

why is validation impossible? Because, we are told in the same document, mystical experience is mediated in specific ways:

"There are NO pure (i.e. unmediated) experiences. Neither mystical experience nor more ordinary forms of experience give any indication, or any grounds for believing, that they are unmediated. That is to say, all experience is processed through, organized by, and makes itself available to us in extremely complex epistemological ways. The notion of unmediated experience seems, if not self-contradictory, at best empty" p. 26.

Everyone would agree that conventional experiences are, in fact, mediated by familiar concepts and expressed in words we have learned. But, everyone who has experienced the mystical state, whether a saint or a heathen, would affirm emphatically that if mystical experiences are mediated at all, they must be mediated by something beyond everyone's knowledge. This is why, the first thing all mystics say is that their experience is ineffable and that when they try, in order to make it understood to themselves and to others, to express it with words and concepts they often end up offering paradoxical statements. Disregarding this fundamental fact about the mystical state, which is what Steven Katz appears to be doing, is a full-proof way of eliminating the possibility not only of its validation but of its existence as well.

In the interest of moving the analysis of the contextualist thesis along, let us not eliminate the peculiarities of the mystical state prematurely. Let us accept that mystical experiences are as extraordinary as every mystic affirms them to be and also accept the fact that they can be and often are approximated by familiar words and culturally–conditioned concepts and beliefs. Now to the degree that these approximations express only the views of the particular culture of the mystic and nothing further, they de facto do not represent aspects or all mystical states but only their particular culturally sanctioned interpretation, exactly as Dr. Katz claims:

"Thus, for example, the nature of the Christian mystic's pre-mystical consciousness informs the mystical consciousness such that he experiences the mystic reality in terms of Jesus, the Trinity, or a personal God, etc., rather than in terms of the non-personal, non-everything, to be precise, Buddhist doctrine of nirvana. Care must also be taken to note that even the plurality of experience found in Hindu, Christian, Muslim, Jewish, Buddhist mystical traditions, etc., have to be broken down into smaller units. Thus we find, for example, in Hinduism monistic, pantheistic, and theistic trends, while Christianity knows both absorptive and non-absorptive forms of mysticism" p. 27.

Moreover, Katz continues, "The Christian mystic usually says that what he experiences is 'union with God'. The Hindu mystic says that his experience is one in which his individual self is identical with Brahman or the Universal Self. The Christian says that his experience supports theism and is not an experience of actual identity with God, and he understands 'union' as not involving identity but some other relation such as resemblance. The Hindu insists on identity, and says that his experience establishes what writers on mysticism usually call 'pantheism'- though Hindus usually do not use that western word. The Buddhist mystic - at least according to some versions of Buddhism - does not speak of God or Brahman or a Universal Self, but interprets his experience in terms which do not include the concept of a Supreme Being at all" p. 29.

It must be obvious to the reader that these are some of the facts that have also been clearly laid out in the previous chapter. But these facts do not preclude other facts. Specifically, they do not preclude that there are additional features which are culture-independent and define with their presence all mystical states no matter in what cultural context the latter arise—something that, paradoxically, the same author has actually admitted three pages earlier:

"what is being argued is that, for example, the Hindu mystic does not have an experience of x which he then describes in the, to him, familiar language and symbols of Hinduism, but rather he has a Hindu experience, i.e. his experience is not an unmediated experience of x but is itself the, *at least partially*, pre-formed anticipated Hindu experience of Brahman. Again, the Christian mystic does not experience some unidentified reality, which he then conveniently labels God, but rather has the *at least partially* prefigured Christian experiences of God, or Jesus, or the like". p. 26 (emphasis mine).

Culture is indeed conditioning the expression of the experiences *but only partially*, which means that part of them is culture-independent. That it is feasible to separate culture-specific features from others that are specific to the way the human cognitive apparatus interacts with reality, is shown by the fact that we have indeed performed that separation in the previous chapter. The procedure I followed was to identify what expressions describing the mystical state varied *systematically* from culture to culture and to reject the corresponding features as not universal or culture-independent aspects of the mystical experience while retaining those that were universal or nearly so. Or, to put it differently, I identified the culture-invariant features by abstracting from the culture specific-expressions the common element that could be discerned in all of them, that element that was not "prefigured"—to use Katz's term—in the rest of the experience, that is, in its culture-specific part.

Only this contextualist, having first asserted that only some aspects of the mystical state are culture-specific (therefore that others are not), does not recognize the legitimacy of the procedure of separating the two classes. He, in fact, finds fault in William James' use of that procedure of abstracting from many diverse descriptions of the mystical experience the feature of noetic quality that is common to them all:

"James has caught something important in calling attention to the noetic element in mystical experience", he opines, "but it is nonetheless not an element that provides the desired commonality. Consider, to begin with, the variety of different knowledge claims which could fit James's definition and which his own examples acknowledge, i.e. this characteristic has been claimed for such differing experiences as those which might be classed as aesthetic, ethical, natural, religious, and mystical. To argue, as James does, that because each such experience claims to give 'insight into depths of truth unplumbed by the discursive intellect' all the experiences are the same, fails to recognize both the variety of 'insights' one could have into the 'depths of truth' and the variety of 'truths', which can lurk in these depths waiting to be 'plumbed'. The variety of claims made for such knowledge of the 'truth' is staggering, running, as they do, from Pythagorean speculations to voodoo, animism, and totemism, to Madame Blavatsky's theosophy and Huxley's and Ramakrishna's philosophia perennis, to say nothing of the variety of more traditional religions" p. 49.

It is indeed possible for someone to attach the predicate "noetic" to Pythagorean speculations, to voodoo, to animism, and totemism, to theosophy and to Huxley's and Ramakrishna's perennial philosophy *and* to the mystical experiences, but that someone would either have to be oblivious of the glaring fact that the predicate was meant to apply *only* to the mystical experiences under discussion or, worse, to assume that James was the one who was ignorant of the proper use of predicates!

Were we to heed it, Katz's criticism would dissuade us from applying the predicate "beautiful" to describe a feature shared by a flock of grazing goats, for example, for fear of offending the "Miss Universe" contestants, or from using the predicate "sinful" in talking about a chocolate dessert, in case someone misunderstood us as implying that pastries are destined to burn in hell.

But possible lapses of the sort exemplified above, occasionally exhibited by its advocate aside, contextualism would appear to have an easier time (although it would ultimately fail—see below) showing that the validity of the genuine features of mystical experiences is impossible to demonstrate if it claimed that the experiences were *totally* as opposed to *partially* prefigured by their several cultural contexts. But to the degree that it claims (and here I assume that all contextualists follow Dr. Katz on this point) that the mystical experiences are only partially thus prefigured, it cannot also claim that their validity is indeterminate.

Moreover, what follows later in this and the next chapter is a concrete demonstration that the validity of mystical experiences can indeed be assessed precisely because part of them is independent of the particular cultures in which they occur and that part reflects something common to all of them, not prefigured by any specific culture. And, that something could well be true of the world beyond the experiencing subject in the way most of our ordinary veridical percepts, sensations and logical inferences are. But let me amplify a bit this important point.

There may be more radical contextualists who, unlike Katz, could claim that the mystical experiences are not "*at least partially* pre-formed" by cultural peculiarities but they are *totally* pre-formed by these cultural peculiarities. I confess that I did not search the literature to the degree that would allow me to verify if and where such claims have been made. But in case they have been or will be made I would like to explain why they would be self-defeating:

If no experience or no part of any experience were conditioned by (or was not reflecting) something beyond the subject's culturally formed mind, every person would be an island; the mind of every person would be incapable of the most elementary form of perception; incapable of learning anything, incapable, therefore, of becoming culturally conditioned and culturally pre-formed! The fact that minds, though culturally conditioned, are conditioned in a way that allows them *to also* contact and interact with aspects of the reality beyond themselves; the fact that we do perceive the world around us, suffices to show the absurdity of the radical contextualist claim.

It appears then that our experiences, the mystical ones included, are in part culturally conditioned and in part are conditioned by the nature of our cognitive apparatus. If they were only culturally conditioned then the contextualists would be right and it would be impossible to assess the validity of any of the features of the mystical state because none of them would be genuine. Given the fact that some of the features of every mystical experience are genuine, the question can be asked as to whether they are delusions of the kind the cognitive apparatus creates under certain circumstances or are objectively true[13].

Normally, we deem any experience such as the notion "two plus two is four" or that a sensation is pleasant or that the shape of the earth is round as being objectively true or false on the basis of some evidence that are appropriate to each notion. Those that have decided that the mystical experience is a delusion support their verdict by appealing to what they consider appropriate evidence to that effect. In the rest of the sections of this chapter, this evidence will be reviewed. And, in the next chapter of the book, evidence to the opposite effect will also be presented in order to enable the uninitiated who are also undecided on this matter to decide what is most reasonable, therefore what they ought to believe[14].

13 To the same conclusion regarding the errors of contextualism lead Wainwright's arguments but from a different direction (see Wainwright, WJ. Mysticism. Sussex: the Harvester Press, 1981)

14 Occasionally, what one believes is also what one ought to believe on the basis of the available evidence. Quite as often, though, even when they are shown the evidence people choose to ignore it if it is in conflict with their worldview—a failing of which hardly anyone is immune.

The General Objection to the Validity of the Mystical State

Outlandish statements are hard to believe; some, absolutely so. No sane person, for instance, would believe that two plus two is five or that the Parthenon was crafted by purposeless and blind natural forces shaping it incrementally over untold millennia. The believability (or absurdity) of other statements is less obvious: Most people living in the dark ages could not be persuaded that the earth on which they treaded is a sphere rotating unsupported in space, and from about the dawn of Enlightenment to the end of the 19th century most literate individuals would be hard-pressed to accept the tales of the mystics as statements of fact: that, for example, out there and all around us lurks a universal Mind or Consciousness of which the individual minds are part, perhaps in the manner drops of ocean spray are part of the ocean or in some other way; that the stardust is more like mind-dust than ordinary dust; that the least disturbance on the world's most remote corner is sensed throughout its space-time extent; that the brain is not a machine that manufactures consciousness but a filter that allows aspects of the universal Mind to become the several streams of personal consciousnesses.

Belief in the absolutely incredible notions, like two plus one is five, is among the marks of psychosis. But most notions seem extravagant only when they are evaluated in the context of a circumambient worldview that clashes with them—something that does not happen with the statement "the sum of two plus two is five". Once this context changes, their extravagance disappears. The previously odd notions become reasonable and believable. This is definitely true of the tales of the mystics. It seems that their bizarreness is due to the fact that they clash with the worldview of the uninitiated. Therefore, recognition of that basic fact and guarding against its influence is a necessary prerequisite for assessing objectively, on the basis of evidence, the truth of these tales.

Of the several verbal renderings of the ineffable object or referent of the mystical knowledge, we have identified, the following appear to be its genuine features: First, its blinding luminosity which, not being a perceptual attribute, may denote the total absence of particulars, that is the unity of all its parts, which is, the second feature of the mystical object and which I attempted to make a bit clearer before, by describing it as a chemical compound and contrasting it with a collection of externally interacting elements. Third, its being akin to mind or consciousness rather than to matter or energy as the latter are commonly defined. Fourth, its being eternal or "beyond space and time". Does such an object actually exist independently of the subjects that experience it, or is it entirely a figment of the mystics' minds?

The subject-independent existence of an object of this sort would be laughed out of court if it was defended in a courtroom full of the most representative scientists humanity had produced from the time of the

Enlightenment to the end of the 19th century. But the situation is different today. Today, a great change in thinking about the nature of the universe and our conception of it has taken place. To quote Arthur Eddington, the noted astrophysicist and philosopher of science, as he saw the situation at the dawn of the 20th century: "It was the boast of the Victorian Physicist that he would not claim to understand a thing until he could make a model of it; and by a model he meant something constructed of levers, geared wheels, squirts, or other appliances familiar to an engineer. At least that is how Nature in building the universe was supposed to be dependent on just the same kind of resources as any human mechanic; and when the physicist sought an explanation of phenomena his ear was straining to catch the hum of machinery. The man who could make gravitation out of cog-wheels would have been a hero in the Victorian age. Nowadays we do not encourage the engineer to build the world for us out of his material, but we turn to the mathematician to build it out of his material. ...*We are dealing in physics with a symbolic world...*" pp. 206–207 (emphasis mine)[15].

In the context of the model of the world before the advent of the new physics the notion of something existing before the beginning of time would be an absurdity because time (and space) were not supposed to have a beginning. Today, in contrast, there is such a thing as "before or beyond time and space"—it is an integral part of modern Cosmology.

The mathematical theory of Chaos, the equations of General Relativity and, more directly still, those of Quantum Mechanics are presenting us a world that does not consist of parts that act and react on each other like billiard balls but one where the, by now proverbial, batting of a butterfly's wings may affect the weather on the other side of the Pacific and where what happens to things here may affect the shape of things on the other end of the universe. Quantum entanglement, to which I just alluded, is by no means a vindication of the mystical knowledge but as certainly it is not incompatible with it as the notions harbored by 19th century science are—notions that have yet to be abandoned by most adherents to the physicalist or the Democritean world legend.

Besides physics, current understanding of the form of unity that would account for the cohesiveness of the components of the ecological system, or the form of unity that guides processes like that of embryogenesis and sustains the cohesiveness of the colonies of cells that constitute organisms and colonies of the organisms that constitute societies of termites or bees is not far from the corresponding mystical insight of "unity".

Even closer compatibility of the mystical vision and that of the new physics is obvious in the conceptions and pronouncements of some of its founders regarding the ultimate constituents of the world. "The reality we can put into words is never reality itself" asserts Werner Heisenberg,

15 Eddington, AS. The nature of the Physical World. London: Dent 1928/1964.

echoing the ancient and contemporary mystics and, more to the point, he adds: "I think that modern physics has definitely decided in favor of Plato. In fact, the smallest units of matter are not physical objects in the ordinary sense; they are forms, ideas which can be expressed unambiguously only in mathematical language"[16].

Max Planck, perhaps *the* founding father of the new physical theory concurs with the opinion that the ultimate constituents of the world are mind-like rather than material: "As a physicist who has devoted his whole life to rational science, to the study of matter, I think I can safely claim to be above any suspicion of irrational exuberance. Having said that, I would like to observe that my research on the atom has shown me that there is no such thing as matter in itself. What we perceive as matter is merely the manifestation of a force that causes the subatomic particles to oscillate and holds them together in the tiniest solar system of the universe. Since there is in the whole universe neither an intelligent force nor an eternal force (mankind, for all its yearnings, has yet to succeed in inventing a perpetual motion machine), we must assume that this force that is active within the atom comes from a conscious and intelligent mind. That mind is the ultimate source of matter"[17].

Mind-like are the ultimate and real constituents of the universe that hide behind the "imaginary" material stuff of our perception according to Eddington as well: "the stuff of the world is mind-stuff" he tells us and explains: "As is often the way with crude statements, I shall have to explain that by 'mind' I do not here exactly mean mind and by 'stuff' I do not at all mean stuff. Still this is about as near as we can get to the idea in a simple phrase. The mind-stuff of the world is, of course, something more general than our individual conscious minds; but we may think of its 'nature' as not altogether foreign to the feelings in our consciousness. The realistic matter and fields of force of former physical theory are altogether irrelevant—except in so far as the mind-stuff has itself spun these imaginings"[18].

These, of course, are opinions that are not shared by all the eminent scientists. Some, like Paul Dirac, were not ready to endorse views such as those of Eddington, of Heisenberg or of Plank. As for the reason I do not quote these dissenting opinions, it is not because I consider them any less rational but because they were not presented as conclusions of arguments but as professions of a creed. In any case, the opinions, whether converging or diverging with the content of mystical knowledge, are not to be taken as evidence vindicating the latter. They are only presented to demonstrate

16 https://www.goodreads.com/author/quotes/64309.Werner_Heisenberg.

17 The German original is as quoted in *The Spontaneous Healing of Belief* (2008) by Gregg Braden, p. 212. "Geist", here translated as "mind" can also be translated as "spirit".

18 Eddington, AS. The Nature of the Physical World p.267.

the movement of contemporary intellectuals away from the Democritean world legend that held absolute sway in physical science until the dawn of the 20th century and the consequent mutation of previously extravagant notions to perfectly reasonable albeit hypothetical ones in the eyes of those that are aware of the great paradigmatic shifts of our times.

Once more, this convergence of the mystical notions and those of the new physical theory *does not* constitute evidence of the subject-independent existence of the objects of the mystical knowledge. What it does, instead, is to remove the veneer of bizarreness and extravagance from the claims of the mystics and to render them no more and no less reasonable than any other hypotheses, to be assessed on the basis of evidence.

Specific Objections to the Validity of the Mystical State

The common theme of the various specific objections to the validity of the mystical state, a sample of which is presented below, is that the experience is the product of a neurophysiological process in the brain, a possibly aberrant or defective one, but in any case, it is a delusion. This theme is founded on one of the central hypotheses of the Democritean world legend, according to which the brain manufactures all experiences. Codified in the work of a psychologist, Leuba, who, in 1925 published what is considered to be a classic scientific study on Mysticism[19] but which is actually a reiteration of the article of the physicalist creed, which was taking over, at that time, continental psychiatry, reduced all facets of human mentation including ethics, religion and, of course, the mystical claims, to brain chemistry.

In the context of that world legend the hypothesis has, over the years, acquired surreptitiously the status of a fact and the inference that all experiences deriving from an aberrant or defective brain process are themselves defective (illusions, delusions or hallucinations) is taken axiomatically to be correct. There is nothing unreasonable with the hypothesis. It could, in fact, be a correct one. It is certainly true that there is a very close correlation between the state of the brain and the type of the corresponding experiences. Some people also entertain the reasonable belief that the correlation is perfect. But no reasonable scientist would, or, at the very least, should, mistake a correlation for a causal relation. The inference, on the other hand, that aberrant physiology must create delusions is simply wrong for reasons to be explained in the remainder of this chapter.

In the following paragraphs, a sample of the most often voiced specific objections to the validity of mystical knowledge will be described in order to demonstrate that none is correct but that each is as likely to be incorrect as it is to be correct. They are summarized under three headings

19 Leuba, J H. The psychology of Religious Mysticism. New York: Harcourt, 1925

according to the presumed cause that renders mystical experiences delusions: Psychopathology, Neuropathology and Aberrant or Atypical brain activity.

Psychopathology

In some respects, the tales of the ancient mystics were quite similar to the tales of those who used psychedelic drugs recreationally and both were sometimes strikingly similar to the musings of schizophrenics. The realization of these similarities led to the free distribution of LSD by the Swiss manufacturer, the Sandoz Company, to psychiatric institutions in Europe and in America to be used for the experimental study of psychosis. The results of this study did not provide evidence that the mystical state is like the psychotic state, neither in terms of symptomatology nor in terms of the underlying neurochemistry, and still have not.

This inconclusiveness, however, does not exclude the possibility that the mystical state is similar to that of psychosis although there are definite dissimilarities between the two: The delusions of schizophrenics are not ineffable but plainly conventional. Psychotic patients "hear" voices conveying very clearly understood messages and "see" visions with equally well-understood content. Mystical experiences are not conventional in that respect and, as it has been repeatedly stated, neither are they sensory or perceptual ones. Mystical experiences are not "visions". Therefore what one could say with reasonable confidence is that the visions associated especially with the onset of drug-facilitated mystical states are similar to some schizophrenic experiences but one could say nothing about the similarity of the mystical state with possible equivalent states that psychotic patients may experience for lack of reliable testimonies to that effect. Moreover, psychotic delusions and hallucinations are chronic, they occur repeatedly rather than rarely, they are mostly spontaneous rather than intended, and, as a rule, they have dysfunctional and often affectively negative repercussions in the life of the patient rather than positive ones, which is mostly the case with the mystical states.

For these reasons alone, it is simply bad science to classify together mystical and psychotic states and then claim that the former are as abnormal and delusional as the latter. But the more basic reason for avoiding such conclusions is that the nature of the brain state associated with an experience is *never* grounds for assessing the validity of the experience—a proposition to be defended, as promised earlier, in the next section. At this point, the only reasonable conclusion is that it is possible that the neurophysiological state of psychosis is similar to that of the mystical state, although the differences in their respective symptomatology seem to point to the opposite direction.

There are, of course, other reasons for believing that the mystical states are delusional. Some of these derive from "depth" psychologies, where mystical experiences are considered symptoms of a variety of alternative and often mutually exclusive unconscious psychical mechanisms. As I have commented before (see chapter 2) and will comment once again, I find such accounts of all psychological phenomena and not only of the mystical experiences, irrelevant to the question of validity, therefore not worthy of systematic refutation. The interested reader, however, may find an informative account of them in the pages of Paul Marshall's recent book[20].

My own reason of dismissing them here is this: None of these "explanations" of depth psychology ever became a verifiable scientific theory. They remained, at best, elaborations of ancient myths and many missed the point of the original formulations of these myths and reduced all behavior and mentation to a handful of ill-defined, purely conjectural psychic mechanisms all of them in principle inaccessible to any form of falsification.

For, certainly, there is no way of deciding, either by experiment or rational argument that the mystical experience is "reparative psychological response to childhood loss" rather than "nostalgia for intra-uterine absorption" or "persistence of infantile ideation in the adult mind"[21] any more than one can decide whether a conventional neurotic symptom is due to repressed urges of copulating with one's mother or some other equally lamentable and unverifiable motive. And, it is interesting to note that all these "theories" emerged as so many fireworks that lit the sky of the twentieth century, a century looking desperately for answers to psychological questions of commensurate significance, novelty and authority to those emerging in Physics, only to fizzle out towards the end of the same century, leaving behind them a lot of smoke and no light.

There is one factor, though, common to all these "theories" that deserves attention because it is relevant to the present discussion: It is the conjecture that all behavior and all human mentation whether conscious, subconscious or unconscious, are produced by the brain. Therefore the symptoms that the mystical states are taken to be in the context of these "theories", are ultimately seen as products of some dysfunction of the brain, therefore non-valid. This conjecture, also adopted by the enthusiasts of the Democritean legend that includes most neuroscientists, psychologists and psychiatrists, does deserve additional consideration given that it implicates causes that are understandable and can be, in principle, identified, examined and assessed. To those, I will now turn.

Neuropathology

So, the proposition goes, the mystical experience is the output of a defective neuronal mechanism. But, as some have suggested, it could also be the

20 Marshall, P. Mystical Encounters with the Natural World. New York: Oxford University Press, 2005.

21 Ibid.

output of a very adaptive brain mechanism; one that has evolved for the purpose of coping with pain and fear that are ubiquitous in this life. This hypothesis would have some merit if the mystical state were to emerge reliably when pain or fear became unbearable, like the "freezing" response of animals in the face of mortal danger. Yet this is not the case. The typical emergence of the mystical state follows elaborate preparation and specific procedures involving either meditation or the use of psychotropic substances and extremely rarely does it follow upon great fear or extreme pain. And, in those cases that it emerges without the mystic's intent, it does so mostly in the context of positive or affectively neutral mood. Nevertheless, the above counterevidence aside, there is a possibility, however remote, that the mystical state is the product of a coping mechanism. Where this possibility viable, its relevance to the issue of the validity would then have to be demonstrated, since the inference "experiences produced by a coping mechanism are delusional" is by no means self-evident.

An alternative hypothesis, entertained by many neuroscientists whether experts in epilepsy or not, is that the mystical state is (or is akin to) an epileptic state. The latter are excused for not appreciating the obvious differences in the symptoms and signs of the two states but the same courtesy can hardly be extended to the experts. "Both the occurrence of paranormal experiences and their rates of incidence are associated with specific types of neuronal activity within the temporal lobes" claims, among others, the late Michael Persinger, possibly the best-known investigator of the neurophysiology of mystical and other, paranormal, states[22].

I would argue that this claim, made by several investigators of whom Dr. Persinger is one, to the degree that it concerns the mystical states, is factually wrong as far as the "rate of incidence" of mystical states goes and unsupported by any evidence as far as the association with "neuronal activity within the temporal lobes" as opposed to any other lobes or parts of lobes goes.

The rate of incidence of mystical states is simply unknown and, today especially, it varies with the rate at which people experiment with psychedelic substances or engage in meditation and there is no evidence of temporal lobe monitoring (especially to the exclusion of the other parts of the brain) while people are experiencing the mystical state. The relevant neuroimaging studies that were (and are currently) performed along with their results will be reviewed later. Yet that review will not alter the fact that no association between mystical experiences and temporal lobe activity has ever been established[23].

22 Persinger, MA. The neuropsychiatry of paranormal experiences. Neuropsychiatric Practice and Opinion. 2001, 13, 515–524.

23 See for example Greyson B, Broshek, DK, Derr LL, Fountain NB. Mystical experiences associated with seizures. Religion, Brain & Behavior, 2015, 5:3, 182–196.

As for the claimed association between temporal lobe seizures and mystical states, it is no more than an over-reaching conjecture and a wrong one at that, based on the fact that temporal lobe epilepsy—the most common type afflicting children and adults—is often associated with experiences called "auras". Why then is the claimed association baseless? In the first place, mystics are not epileptics. No doubt, among the hundreds of thousands or millions who have experienced the mystical state through the millennia and the thousands who are currently experiencing it around the world, some might have been epileptics as others may have sustained head injuries, brain cysts, tumors, arteriovenous malformations, hydrocephalus and other dreaded maladies involving the temporal and the rest of the brain lobes. But there is no evidence whatsoever indicating that any sample of mystics differs in that respect from any other sample of the world population.

In fact, as anyone can verify by browsing the websites of the major centers where experimentation with psychedelics is now pursued, the volunteers selected for such studies, a good proportion of whom do attain the mystical state, are screened for both neurological and psychiatric disorders. And, yes, it is true that electrical stimulation of a particular area in the temporal lobe[24] and the parietal lobe[25] can produce the "out of body experience" but out of body experiences are not the same as mystical experiences even if in some cases they occur in the context of the mystical state.

It is also true that some epileptic seizures are preceded by auras, that is, by very definite experiences, mostly sensory and very unlike the mystical states in several fundamental ways. In extremely rare occasions, though, an aura may be strikingly similar to a mystical experience. One such example is provided in Dostoevfky's "The Idiot" in a passage where the author describes his own experiences, as an epileptic, although he attributes them to his novel's hero, Prince Myshkin:

"...suddenly, in the midst of sadness, spiritual darkness and oppression, there seemed at moments a flash of light in his brain, and with extraordinary impetus all his vital forces suddenly begun working at their highest tension. The sense of life, the consciousness of self, were multiplied ten times at these moments which passed like a flash of lightning. His mind and his heart were flooded with extraordinary light; all his uneasiness, all his doubts, all his anxieties were relieved at once: they were all merged in a lofty calm, full of serene, harmonious joy and hope...These moments were only an extraordinary quickening of self-consciousness...for this moment (he said) one may give one's whole life...at that moment (he seemed)

24 "Persinger, M. A. Modern neuroscience and near-death experiences: Expectancies and implications. Comments on "A neurobiological model for near-death experiences." Journal of Near-Death Studies, 1989, 7, 233–239."

25 Beauregard, M. "Near Death Explained" Salon. http://www.salon.com/2012/04/21/near_death_explained

to understand the extraordinary saying that *there shall be no more time*" pp. 208–209 (parentheses mine)[26].

Is then, Prince Mishkin's aura a mystical state? Personally, I am inclined to accept it as such but several arguments can be marshaled against this inclination: Unlike mystical experiences, auras like the one described by Dostoevfsky are different for different patients. Some are pleasant but others are not. Even in the blissful ones of the kind just recounted it is unclear whether the level of the mystical bliss is reached. Neither the pleasant nor the unpleasant ones are ineffable and otherworldly. None is reported, as far as I know, to feature "undifferentiated union" or any other sort of union with the totality of existence; or to feature the Uncreated Light; or to have resulted in long-term improvements of the patients' psychological health and social conduct.

The light that flooded Prince Myshkin's mind, was not necessarily the otherworldly Light of the mystical state but a metaphorical expression of relief from conventional anxieties. Even the statement that "there shall be no more time", that may remind one of the "timelessness" of the mystical object, it may mean nothing of the sort as it may refer instead to John the Evangelist's contention that there is no time left before the final act of the Divine Will[27].

In spite of these objections, I will assume that Dostoevsky's aura is sufficiently similar to a typical mystical state to qualify as one. I will further assume that such incidents where the epileptic aura brings about the mystical state exist and that many of them may have gone unreported. What would be unreasonable to accept, on the other hand, is that such incidents form a corpus considerable enough for the case to be made that mystical states are epileptic auras. And, it is unreasonable in view of the additional fact that unlike auras that repeat reliably albeit unexpectedly over time, in order for mystical states to be elicited, the expenditure of mental effort or the aid of drugs is required.

It is therefore fair to conclude that some mystical states may be triggered by epileptic activity in the brain although in most instances epileptic activity does not trigger mystical states. But could all mystical states be triggered by brain states *similar* to epileptic ones? They certainly might: the linkage between epilepsy and the mystical state Dr. Persinger alluded to may have been meant as merely one of similarity. "This linkage" Persinger writes "... simply indicates that specific patterns of activity within the temporal lobes and related structures are associated with the experiences. The sources of the stimuli that evoke the neuroelectrical changes may range from properties intrinsic to chaotic activity, with minimal veridicality, to external information that is processed by mechanisms not known to

26 Dostoevfsky, F. The Idiot. New York: Barnes & Noble books, 1868/2004.

27 See The New Testament: Revelations 10,6.

date". p. 515[28] and for a good measure he adds the historical untruth that many adherents of the physicalist world legend like to propound: "God experiences, which are often employed as proofs of god beliefs, are likely to have been responsible for more human carnage in the history of civilization than any single pestilence" p. 519[29].

Although we may not expect from neuroscientists and psychologists historical expertise, it is only fair to expect of them precise statement of their positions when the latter fall within range of their expertise: In the first place, some pattern of brain activation involving not only the temporal lobe but other areas as well *is bound to exist* while *any* and *every* experience transpires. *The question is whether there is something in these patterns (other than epileptic discharges, this time), which alerts the expert brain-activity-pattern-decipherer that the experience is true or false.* To this question, we do not have an explicit answer in the quotation above. What we have instead is the innuendo that something of the sort that is presently unknown but will be discovered in the future will inform the expert brain-activity-pattern-gazer that the experiences must be delusions. But, that this expectation, even if it does transpire, is utterly irrelevant to the truth or falsehood of the mystical experiences will be demonstrated in the next section.

Atypicality

Aberrant brain states can be either merely infrequent or abnormal, like those associated with excessive stress brought about by the practices of infliction of severe pain and by a number of mental disorders. Now it is a useful habit of thought to treat rare and aberrant mental and behavioral events that are radically different from conventional ones as delusions, illusions and hallucinations because in most cases this is precisely what they prove to be.

Carried away by the force of this habit, one may also consider the brain activity associated with mystical experiences as non-valid aberration by virtue of the rarity of the corresponding experiences and their radical difference from conventional ones. On the basis of criteria such as this, however, all breakthrough experiences, all insights departing radically from ordinary thoughts that mark scientific or artistic innovations should also be classified as delusional, and the brain activity associated with them should be deemed aberrant or abnormal. For that reason alone rarity and a-typicality are not grounds for attributing to any experience, mystical or otherwise, lack of validity. But the more fundamental reason not to be carried away by habitual patterns of thought will be discussed in the next section.

28 Persinger, MA. The neuropsychiatry of paranormal experiences. Neuropsychiatric Practice and Opinion. 2001, 13, 515–524.

29 Ibid.

Also, force of habit leads to the false conclusion that since particular drugs are definitely associated with mystical states, the latter are nothing but the false experiences resulting from temporary excess or lack of a particular chemical, in this case possibly excess of serotonin or something that acts like serotonin, in the brain, lasting as long as this chemical imbalance prevails. Once again, the fact that a chemical can induce a change in behavior and mentation—a fact expected of many chemicals in the first place—has nothing to say about the truth or falsity of the resulting behavior or experience as it will be explained in the next section.

Force of habit again, that is to say, thinking as if the Democritean world legend were God's absolute truth, leads to the following non-sequitur: "We now have concrete evidence, provided by functional neuroimaging, that clearly visible patterns of brain activity are associated with, therefore produce, the mystical states, therefore (again) mystical states must be delusional. Before showing the irrelevance of the above double inference, let us take a brief look at the nature of these studies.

They all aim at identifying the pattern of brain activity that corresponds to the mystical state with the further aim of claiming that the mystical state is the result of the pattern of activity. To achieve the first aim one has to manage things so that the people whose brain activity pattern is recorded do, in fact, experience the state. (In the next section I will lay out the basic concepts involved in such recordings with the modern functional imaging methods). This is a very demanding task so that in some of the early studies[30] the investigators settled for recording the brain pattern of nuns while the latter were *remembering their mystical union with God*. But even if the "union with God" was a genuine mystical state, its recollection, which is a conventional experience, is a fundamentally different affair than the original unconventional mystical experience. Consequently whatever pattern was recorded in that and similar studies not involving a genuine mystical state is irrelevant to the present discussion.

Subsequently, investigators took that lesson to heart and recorded brain activity while their volunteers were experiencing drug-facilitated mystical states—verified by their responses to the appropriate questionnaires. In one such study[31], the pattern recorded was characterized by decreased activity in the thalamus, the cingulate gyrus and the medial prefrontal cortex and also decreased coupling (to be also explained in the next section) between the cingulate and the medial prefrontal cortex.

Other studies, however, have disclosed a pattern featuring increased rather than decreased activity in the medial frontal and no changes in the prefrontal cortex. Still other studies have identified patterns featuring

30 e.g. Beauregard M, Paquette V. Neural correlates of a mystical experience in Carmelite nuns. Neuroscience Letters. 2006, 405, 186–190.

31 Carhart-Harris et al. Neural correlates of the psychedelic state as determined by fMRI studies with psilocybin. PNAS 2012,(6) 2138–2143.

increases in the lateral parietal cortex but not in the medial, while additional ones have found decreases in the same vicinity[32].

The variability in the identified patterns should not come as a surprise. This form of research involving functional neuroimaging is still developing and many factors that have not been identified yet exert their influence on the results. At this point, announcements to the contrary notwithstanding, the pattern of brain activity that corresponds to the mystical state has *not* been identified. But undoubtedly, sooner or later, it will. And, when it does, we will know what areas form the particular network the activity of which corresponds to the mystical state. We will most likely also find what neurotransmitters are used in the creation of that activity pattern and will then understand better the role of the psychedelics in its creation.

Moreover, some of us will undoubtedly go beyond what the scientific data show us and draw the metaphysical inference[33] that we have discovered the pattern that not only corresponds to but also creates the mystical state. In the next section, I will demonstrate why even the acceptance of this metaphysical conclusion in no way justifies the claim that the mystical state thus created has no objective validity. I will also show that even if the various claims reviewed to the effect that some pathological or aberrant activity in the brain triggers or creates the mystical state, the inference that, for this reason, the states are delusional, is a false inference.

Brain Activity Patterns and Experiences

In the previous sections of this chapter, it was shown that for a variety of reasons the alternative explanations of mystical states as subjective delusions (either because they may be triggered by epileptic activity or other brain lesions or by psychotic-like symptoms or merely because they are atypical and rare) are either 1 more likely to be wrong or 2, as likely to be wrong as to be right. It is now time to explain why even if mystical experiences were the result of abnormal discharges of the temporal lobes or of malfunctioning of the brain in general due to lesions or due to neurochemical anomalies associated with some psychopathological condition or due to any other unaccountable or random misfiring of cortical neurons, that fact would be irrelevant to the issue of their validity. As irrelevant, indeed, as is the fact that they are associated with the presence of particular chemical substances and with particular brain activation patterns and equally irrelevant even if they were the very products of these aberrant

32 For a review see Barrett FS and Griffiths RR Classic Hallucinogens and mystical experiences: Phenomenology and Neural Correlates. Curr. Topics Behav. Neurosci. 2017, 36: 393–430.

33 I remind, here, the reader that metaphysical and metaphysics refers refer to statements or theories that cannot be falsified or verified by the empirical data. In this case all relevant data reveal only a correspondence or correlation and not a causal relation.

patterns. To understand why this is the case, a few words regarding the brain activation patterns, what they consist of and how they are recorded with the modern functional neuroimaging devices would be helpful.

To begin with, all cortical neurons are always active, that is, they are always communicating, each using one or more of the different neurotransmitter molecules, like serotonin. The form of communication is therefore chemical but also electrical and this exchange of electrochemical signals constitutes the most basic form of brain activity. When groups of neurons in different parts of the brain are executing a particular function (moving, speaking, emoting, thinking, etc.) the rate at which they exchange signals is increasing, as compared to the rates of other neurons not engaged in the execution of the function. In some cases, engagement in a particular function entails decreasing the basic rate of signaling in some groups of neurons (or brain areas). This difference in the rate of signaling within the areas engaged in the function constitutes the activity pattern specific to that particular function and the set of areas thus engaged is called the brain mechanism of the function or the functional network.

Besides the amount of activity that differentiates the one brain mechanism from the next is the degree to which the exchange of signals is coordinated among the areas that comprise that mechanism or functional network. The degree of this coordination is assessed with several different mathematical procedures called measures of the connectivity of the network. The patterns of electrochemical signaling specific to different behavioral and psychological functions is captured in images using the method of Magnetoencephalography or MEG.

Different rates of exchange of signals characterizing the areas that are parts of a particular network are associated with different rates of consumption of glucose and oxygen by the neurons of the network. Were we to picture these differential rates that characterize an active network we would see a pattern similar to that formed by the electrochemical signaling. Such "metabolic" patterns of activity are captured using the method of Positron Emission Tomography or PET.

But when the degree of metabolic activity differs between the active network and the rest of the brain, so does the rate at which the active areas of the network are supplied with fresh, oxygenated, blood that caries the fuel of the engaged neurons, namely glucose and oxygen. These differential rates of blood supply also form a pattern similar to the electrochemical and the metabolic one for the same network and this pattern is captured in functional images through the use of either the method of PET or the method of functional Magnetic Resonance Imaging or fMRI[34].

34 For a detailed account of these methods and their clinical and research applications see e.g. Papanicolaou, AC. et al. the Oxford Handbook of Functional Brain Imaging in Neuropsychology and Cognitive Neurosciences. Oxford University Press, 2017.

With these methods of functional imaging, it has been possible, thus far, to capture brain activity patterns that correspond to the networks of some simple sensory and motor functions. But with the rapid progress made in the area of functional neuroimaging several more "higher" functional networks like that of language have been partially identified and there is no doubt that many more will be revealed in the not too distant future. Moreover, there is little doubt that the patterns associated with the presumed products of psychological functions, that is, the experiences, will also be pictured as well, even if only incompletely[35].

To this prediction, there is hardly anyone, whether an enthusiast of the Democritean or the hidden world legend, who would object, because there is a universal assumption that to each experience, of any kind whatsoever, corresponds a specific pattern of brain activation, whether or not that type of pattern has or has not been or even whether can or cannot be imaged. Moreover, as mentioned at the closing of the previous section, those who consider the Democritean legend true, interpret the correspondence of patterns and experiences causally, with the pattern being the cause and the experience being the effect.

It follows, therefore, that like all experiences, the mystical ones have a brain correlate as well: a particular activation pattern, or are the results of that activation pattern. But an experience, whether conventional or mystical, cannot be considered delusional or hallucinatory merely because it is a product of electrochemical processes in the brain, unless we are prepared to consider all conscious experiences epiphenomenal, as many people do. Now, "epiphenomenal", formally speaking, means a phenomenon that does not have any causal efficacy; that cannot be the cause of anything; that is, superfluous, and in that sense "fake". Yet even the "epiphenomenalists" agree that since experiences correspond to "real" phenomena, in this case to brain activity patterns, some of those patterns will correspond to valid experiences and some to "false" experiences like illusions hallucinations and delusions: experiences that are not valid.

Calling an experience valid, in this context, is normally meant that the experience, if it is a percept, it is a veridical one rather than an illusion or hallucination and if it is a thought or an inference it is a correct thought or a correct inference as opposed to a logically incorrect one. The question consequently becomes: is there any mark of feature of activation patterns that would allow one to classify the corresponding experience as valid or not valid, as true or false? If there is, then those that claim that mystical experiences are not valid, all they have to do in order to convince those that are agnostic on the issue of believe the opposite, is to point at this feature or mark in the corresponding pattern.

35 Ibid. see especially Chapters 9–11.

Clearly, though, this is impossible since we have yet to identify experience-specific patterns in sufficient detail to even differentiate one type of experience from another type, let alone to discern the marks in the pattern that identify the experience as true or false, valid or not valid. Therefore, at present, those that claim that the mystical experiences are not valid because they may result from aberrant brain activity patterns, simply express an opinion not based on evidence but on their metaphysical belief that this is so and cannot be otherwise. That is, they express an opinion that, objectively, could be correct or, as easily, incorrect.

In which case the question becomes: When the time comes and sufficiently detailed images of patterns corresponding to different types of experiences are available could we then see in them the mark of validity or lack of validity of the corresponding experience? Could, for example the pattern corresponding to the notion "2+2=4" have a feature reassuring us that the notion is valid whereas the pattern corresponding to the notion "2+2=5" have a different one indicating that the notion is not valid?

"Of course it could" is one answer, "because, after all, something in the pattern should, according to the universally accepted assumption, correspond to our subjective experience or feeling of correctness in the one case and something else should correspond to the definitely different feeling of incorrectness, in the other case". But whoever answers thus, misses entirely the point. True, there should be and very likely is a clear difference in the marks contained in the two activity patterns. *But the only way to recognize their respective meaning is to examine the subjective feelings and then associate the one mark with the feeling or correctness and the other mark with the feeling of incorrectness and not the other way round.*

The same argument and the same inescapable conclusion is to be found in James[36], in Dostoevsky's novel, quoted earlier, and very likely in the work of many others who have thought this issue through.

It is therefore certain that the basis of deciding if an experience, conventional or mystical is valid or not, is not the brain activity associated with it but some other criterion—which is something we do anyway when we say, for example, that a "spike and wave pattern" in the electroencephalogram is indicative of epilepsy or a lesion in the primary motor area of the brain is indicative of paresis: It is because we have *already* established on the basis of behavior or mentation that the first is usually associated with epilepsy and the second with paresis that we can *subsequently* recognize them as marks of health or disease.

Accordingly, unless we settle the issue of the validity or lack of validity of the mystical experience on some grounds other than on the fact that

36 James W. The varieties of religious experience: a study in human nature: being the Gifford lectures on natural religion delivered at Edinburgh in 1901–1902, {chapter on Mysticism, 1st chapter}.

they are associated with, or even depend on, brain activation patterns, we cannot classify them as valid or not valid merely because they are so associated or dependent, or because the brain activation patterns are aberrant in one way or another. Such signs of aberration, once again, are irrelevant to the question of validity of the experiences until they are proven to be relevant on the basis of some other criterion.

With this comment, we have reached the end of the inquiry as to whether mystical experiences are delusions and we can conclude that none of the attempts (mostly on the part of ardent followers of the physicalist world legend) at showing that they are delusions *have been successful or even relevant.*

6 The Experiencing Subject and Mystical Object

Defining the Validity of the Mystical State

The Validity of the Genuine Features of the Mystical State

The Validity of the Experience Itself

We have separated the genuine features into three classes: first, features that are intrinsic to the experience itself; second, features that could be attributed either to the experience itself or to the object of the experience and, third, features attributed to the object of the experience. For reasons already offered, we will be considering the features of the first and second set as belonging to the experience qua experience. These are (1) transiency, (2) authoritative or incontestable knowledge of something real but ineffable, of something that is beyond the experiencing subject, (3) passivity marked by the absence of personal will and (4) certainty of a contact or interaction between the self and the ineffable object and the knowing self. The three additional genuine features that may belong either to the object or to the experience itself and are included here are (5) the positive affective state of benevolence or bliss or serenity and the feeling of implicit trust, (6) fearlessness or unconcern even about the certainty of death and other evils and (7) awe.

Are these seven genuine features of the experience valid? They appear to be so on the basis of the two criteria mentioned in the beginning of chapter 5 for judging the validity of these particular features, that is, first, the conviction of the experiencing subject about their validity and, second, their practical consequences. The first, clearly articulated by Franz Brentano whom James quotes approvingly, applies equally to conventional and to mystical experiences: "The phenomena inwardly apprehended are true in themselves. As they appear—of this the evidence with which they are apprehended is a warrant—so they are in reality...No one can doubt whether the psychic condition he apprehends in himself *be* and be *so* as he apprehends it. Whoever should doubt this would have reached that *final* doubt which destroys itself in destroying every fixed point from which to make an attack upon knowledge" pp. 187[1].

1 James, W. Principles of Psychology, Vol I. New York: Cosimo Classics, 1890/2007.

The percept of a mirage, for example, as much as any other percept, is true and real as far as its being an experience goes. And, like any other percept, it can be veridical or not when judged against other experiences, as for instance, against the percept of the same stretch or road that from afar looked flooded, seen from up close. If there is a preponderance of counter-evidence (i.e. the additional experiences), then the belief in the original percept is withheld. But in the absence of such counter-evidence, the original experience is accepted as valid. This of course means that some experiences are believed as true although they are not if we have not found any counter-evidence—a point to be kept in mind for subsequent discussion in the concluding section. Now, all seven features that define the mystical state itself are either felt or not felt, and if they are felt, they are true and real for the subject that experiences them. Therefore, in the absence of any counter-evidence one must conclude that as far as this criterion of veridicality goes, the mystical state is true in the way all sensations and sentiments are true.

In addition, the mystical state can be judged as being true or false in the sense of being justifiable or not on the basis of its consequences, that is, according to the pragmatic criterion that James proposed and defended[2]. And on the basis of that, second, criterion, these features are also true or justified by their long-lasting effects that have been mentioned on several occasions in the previous pages[3].

There is one genuine feature, though, that merits special attention. It is the feature of encounter or interaction of the experiencing subject with the object of the experience; the feature that Stace calls "undifferentiated union"—an appellation I intentionally avoided because it appears to me not to be entirely justified by all the relevant data.

One source of difficulty (already recognized and commented on before) is precisely the lack of reliable evidence, that is, relevant testimony as to whether this contact or the interaction happens during the mystical state whereby the subject's self, mind or soul or consciousness unites with the universal Self or Mind or Soul or Consciousness and remains united as long as the state endures, or whether the experience is simply a *revelation* of an eternal union that has been already effected; actually, effected before the beginning of time.

Another source of difficulty, again due to lack of relevant evidence, is whether the subject's mind is (or becomes) *part* of the Universal Mind or is *identical* with It. But as I announced in the introductory chapter, I refuse to engage in metaphysical speculation in the absence of clear and reliable

2 James, W. On Pragmatism. In William James Writings 1902–1910. Library of America. Literary Classics of the United States, Inc., 1987.

3 A broader criterion that includes the pragmatic one of James is enunciated in Plato's Philebus where the relative merits of knowledge and pleasure are compared.

testimony. Nevertheless, as far as the feature of some sort of contact or interaction is concerned, I believe that it meets the aforementioned two criteria. Therefore it must be admitted that some sort of encounter of an unknown nature is felt to transpire. We can therefore conclude that the features of the mystical state itself are real and true, and they *ought* to be believed to be such.

The Validity of the Object of the Mystical Knowledge

There are many theorems in Logic and Mathematics the proof of which is utterly inaccessible to most people. Equally inaccessible is the internal consistency of some mathematical laws of physics, as for example the one describing the extremely counter-intuitive phenomenon of quantum entanglement. In fact, the proportion of people in the world today that have direct and secure knowledge of the truth of such theorems and of the internal consistency of quantum formalisms is much smaller than the proportion of mystics within the same population. It is highly unlikely that these two samples of humanity would differ in terms of the honesty, reliability and mental health of their respective members. Therefore there should be no reason to doubt that both the experts and the mystics are equally trustworthy.

Let then those of us that do not belong in either group imagine the following announcement from a source we implicitly trust regarding quantum entanglement: "several experts from around the world claim that there is a mathematical formalism that predicts that if a property of one of two twin particles generated at the same time by a machine so as to be identical, is changed here on earth the corresponding property of its twin will change at the same time, even if the twin has traveled by the time the changes were made to the other end of the known universe".

I would imagine that most people will note that there is no way to actually conduct such an experiment that would verify the simultaneous change in the property of the traveling twin the moment its twin on earth was manipulated. But I would also trust that most people would accept that the phenomenon is true or real once they were reassured that all experts in this area of science have mathematical proof and many empirical verifications in relevant laboratory experiments that, if the experiment that was described in the announcement were to actually be done, the predicted phenomenon would happen.

This supposition is based on the common observation that people do believe that logicians and mathematicians have valid knowledge of the truth of theorems they and they alone can prove. It would be a strange occurrence indeed if any normal human being were to declare "I do not believe in Gödel's Incompleteness theorem nor in the Law of Quadratic Reciprocity nor the Pythagorean theorem unless I could prove them myself and I don't care if all the mathematicians of the world bet their lives that they are true".

There is a good reason that whoever was to make such a statement should be considered a bit paranoid. And the reason is that all of us know what it means to be absolutely certain of something—say of the fact that 2+2 is 4 and not 5. And unless we have reason to suspect fraud, we are ready to recognize the same certainty about such things in others who, unlike us, are in a position to know of what they speak. Moreover, we extend the courtesy of accepting the testimony of the experts regarding the truth of all notions vouched by all of them as we accept unconditionally our own testimony about notions that we ourselves know they are true beyond any doubt, such as the notion "A=A" or "2+2=4". Consequently, not extending the same consideration to mystics regarding the validity of what all of them believe unconditionally is a sign of unreasonable bias motivated not by any factual counter-indications but by simple metaphysical preconceptions.

Does this mean that the convictions of mystics and of experts are infallible on issues on which they agree among themselves? We have answered this question in the negative a few paragraphs ago: Convictions on which either all the experts or all the mystics concur are to be treated as true unless counter-evidence falsifies them. For example, the unshakable conviction of Christian mystics that they become one with the Creator may not be (and was not) treated as true due to the presence of counter-evidence in the form of equally incontestable convictions supplied by other mystics to the effect that the union is with both the Creation and the Creator combined.

One should therefore ask: is there any counter-evidence to the claim that the object of the mystical knowledge is eternal and mind-like rather than matter- or physical energy-like? Having accepted the trustworthiness of the witness and their mental health and having shown that any aberrant patterns of activity their brain may display while they are having a mystical experience is irrelevant to the truth-status of that experience, the only "counter-evidence" left is not at all evidence but a metaphysical view that rejects a priori the possibility that the mystical knowledge is true. Accordingly, what one ought to conclude if one is to remain logically consistent requires no further comment.

The Independent Existence of the Mystical Object

Now, their unquestionable truth aside, mathematical and logical "objects" are by no means proven to exist independently of the particular minds that entertain them. It is true that some philosophers, both old and new, starting with Plato, do offer metaphysical arguments in favor of the independent existence of the universals, but it is also true that others argue that the opposite is the case. It is important to note here that believing a universal to be true (e.g. A=A) does not imply endorsement of any particular ontological status for that universal. The universal can exist only in the minds of the people that think it or it can exist independently of the minds that think it, just as Plato proposed.

The situation is altogether different when the issue at stake is not the subject-independent existence of universals but the subject-independent existence of the object or the referent of mystical knowledge. Once the truth of the mystical knowledge is accepted on the same grounds as that of the universals, the subject-independent existence of the mystical object is inadvertently also asserted. And this is why:

Mystical knowledge is, we have said, the awareness of something *beyond the experiencing subject*, which is also timeless and mind-like. Having accepted this knowledge as true on the same grounds one accepts the truth of the universals, one cannot then go back and *selectively disbelieve* any one of the defining features of that object of knowledge for there is no empirical grounds, no counter-evidence in the relevant testimonies, that would justify such a selective disbelief. Once again, the only counter-evidence encountered was the systematically varying features across different groups of mystics. Accordingly, these features were selectively disbelieved and were eliminated. Therefore, once the truth of the contents of mystical knowledge is asserted, it would be capricious or simply irrational to then deny the truth of the feature of independent existence of the object of that knowledge; that is to say, deny the awareness of the mystical object *existing beyond the experiencing subject.*

Would the situation change if we were to follow professor Stace and accept as a genuine feature of the experience the awareness of "undifferentiated unity" rather than the awareness of something beyond the experiencing subject? Not really. In that event, we would first have to further decide whether the union was already effected since before space-time begun to exist and the experience is simply the awareness of that fact, or whether the experience is awareness of the union materializing only during the mystical state.

In the first case, acceptance of the truth of the mystical experience would entail accepting that both the subject and the object have existed and will exist together forever. In the second case, acceptance of the truth of the mystical experience would entail affirmation of the existence of the object—Koestler's ocean—with which the subjective mind, or the self, or consciousness would unite loosing thereby its distinctiveness. Consequently, in both cases, the subject-independent existence of the object of mystical knowledge would be affirmed. But what exactly is that which exists, the empirical data offer no clue beyond the fact that it is timeless and mind-like rather than matter-like.

To reiterate, this conclusion is not any longer at odds with contemporary physical theory and it is partly supported by the opinions of some—albeit not all—the founders of the new physical science. It is not a conclusion of overwhelming persuasiveness, to be sure, but on what grounds would one dismiss it as unsound? I mean, on the strength of what sort of counter-evidence? Well, there is no more counter-evidence left to consider. All known alternative interpretations of mystical knowledge as fake or delusional, starting with the possibility of its being an instance of fraudulent reporting or conscious or unconscious biases on the part of the mystics or a matter of psychological and neurological pathology were found either wrong or irrelevant.

True enough, there is always a possibility, however remote, that there may be counter-evidence that has not yet been discovered. But this possibility does not constitute grounds for suspending belief until and unless such evidence materializes. If it did, no judgment would ever be made on any empirical proposition whatsoever and no experience would ever be believed as being true and valid.

The only grounds, then, for dismissing the conclusion to which the evidence points is the metaphysical preconception that overrides, when we let it override, both empirical evidence and rational argument: the creed of the Democritean world legend which, while receding rapidly from physics and mathematics, still holds sway over the rest of the sciences.

The blinding power of either world legend is not to be underestimated. William James[4] cautioned that long-established and well-entrenched beliefs held either consciously or unconsciously, impede acceptance of new evidence in proportion to the degree the evidence threatens to overthrow their sway[5]. Believing is after-all a powerful affective and not only rational affair[6]. It was the irrationality of some beliefs embedded in the perennial legend that had outgrown their utility or had over-extended their dominion over humanity that brought about the Enlightenment. Perhaps a new Enlightenment where the perennial legend of a hidden world, purged by its rival, of all sorts of offending accretions that have accumulated through the long and dark Middle Ages and that even now distort its message, will once again invigorate scientific and philosophical discourse.

But for that to happen the conclusions of the relevant inquiries must be wholeheartedly accepted and internalized—a feat extremely difficult to accomplish since conclusions of inquiries with wide and deep repercussions in one's life are seldom compelling. There is always a residue of doubt regarding their integrity, born of implicit fear of error, even in the minds of those who see no fault in them and who are unable to offer counter-arguments. Out of this quandary, two diverging roads have been discerned

4 James, W. The Will to Believe and Other Essays in Popular Philosophy. New York: Dover Publications, Inc., 1897/1956.

5 Incidentally, the same notion is embedded in the logic of those statistical approaches where prior beliefs condition the probability of acceptance of subsequent statements.

6 This is why many times there is a tension between what we believe and what we know *we ought* to believe.

since ancient times: the one is favored by religious propagandists, jurists and politicians. It relies on appeals to sentiment, through rituals, incantations, supplications or relentless reassertions of the conclusion to be adopted that embellish and sublimate it, thus rendering its truth inescapable. The efficacy of this method, like that of all methods that capitalize on affect depends on one's attitudes and inclinations. For some, it is the royal road to wisdom and salvation. For others, it is but a trackless wilderness.

The second road is the one bequeathed to us by Socrates, hours before downing the hemlock, at the closing of his arguments for the immortality of the soul. One of his friends and interlocutors, Simmias of Megara, though he had accepted the integrity of the argument, he had yet to bring himself to unconditionally internalizing its truth. He, too, was afraid that his week, all too human, intellect might betray him into committing wholeheartedly to a possibly wrong belief on an issue of such capital importance. He therefore confessed that much to Socrates who replied: "not only this (the conclusion) but the initial axioms, even if you have believed in them, you must examine again and again for greater lucidity. And if you do so sufficiently, I trust that you will comprehend the arguments to the degree it is humanly possible. And if they do become clear to you, you need not search any further"[7] because, as Socrates believed, the moment Logos reaches the pinnacle of its persuasive efficacy, the human mind lets itself slip effortlessly and rest serenely in the affect-laden waters of absolute conviction and Wisdom.

7 Plato, Phaedo (107 b): Ού μονον γε....αλλά και τας υποθέσεις τας πρώτας, και ει πισταί υμίν εισιν, όμως επισκεπτέαι σαφέστερον* και εάν αυτάς ικανώς διέλητε, ως εγώμαι, ακολουθήσατε τω λόγω καθ' όσον δυνατόν μάλιστ' ανθρώπω επακολουθήσαι˙ κάν τούτο αυτό σαφές γένηται, ουδέν ζητήσετε περαιτέρω.

References

Aurobindo, S. The Life Divine. New York: Arya Publishing House, 1949, 139, Vol. I.

Archimandrite Sophrony of Essex. St. Silouan the Athonite.(Greek translation). Essex: Editions of the Holy Monastery of St. John. 8th Edition, 1999.Aurobindo, S. The Life Divine. Arya Publishing House, 1949, 139, Vol. I.

Barrett, FS, Bradstreet, MP, Leoutsakos, JMS, Johnson, MW, and Griffiths, RR. The challenging experience questionnaire: Characterization of challenging experiences with psilocybin mushrooms. Journal of Psychopharmacology. 2016, 30(12), 1279–1295.

Barrett, FS, and Griffiths, RR. Classic hallucinogens and mystical experiences: Phenomenology and neural correlates. Current Topics in Behavioral Neurosciences, 2018, 36, 393–430.

Beauregard, M. "Near Death Explained" Salon. http://www.salon.com/2012/04/21/near_death_explained

Beauregard, M, and Paquette, V. Neural correlates of a mystical experience in Carmelite nuns. Neuroscience Letters. 2006, 405, 186–190.

Bergson, H. Matter and Memory. (N. M. Paul & W. S. Palmer, Trans.). New York: Dover Publications, 1912.

Berkeley, GA. Treatise Concerning the Principles of Human Knowledge. Indianapolis: Hackett Publishing Company, 1710/1982.

Blackmore, S. Dying to Live: Near Death Experience. Buffalo, NY: Prometheus, 1993.

Blanke, O, Ortigue, S, Landis, T, and Seeck, M. Stimulating illusory own-body perceptions. Nature Brief Communications. 2002, 419(19) SEPTEMBER pp 269–270.

Bucke, RM. Cosmic Consciousness: A Study in the Evolution of the Human Mind. New York: E.P. Dutton and Company, Inc., 1901.

Carhart-Harris, et al. Neural correlates of the psychedelic state as determined by fMRI studies with psilocybin. Proceedings of the National Academy of Sciences of the United States of America. 2012, (6), 2138–2143.

Charalambidis, EC. The experience of Uncreated Light in the lives of Athonite saints. University of Thessaloniki, Greece, Doctoral Dissertations, 1999.

de Chardin, PT. The Phenomenon of Man. New York: Harper and Row, 1959.

Dostoevfsky, FF. The Idiot. New York: Barnes & Noble books, 1868/2004.

Eckhart, M. A Modern Translation. Translated by R.B. Blakney. New York and London: Harper and Brothers, 1941.

Eddington, AS. The Nature of the Physical World. London: Dent, 1928/1964.

Franklin, J. A spiritual biography: An account of spiritual/religious experiences from a small child to the present moment. De Numine. 2000, 28.

Garcia-Romeu, A, Griffiths, RR, and Johnson, MW. Psilocybin-occasioned mystical experiences in the treatment of tobacco addiction. Current Drug Abuse Reviews. 2014, 7(3), 157–164.

Grayson, B. "Seeing Dead People Not Known to Have Died: "Peak in Darien" Experiences." American Anthropological Association. November 21, 2010. http://onlinelibrary.wiley.com/doi/10.1111/j.1548-1409.2010.01064.x/abstract.

Greyson, B. Comments on 'Does paranormal perception occur in near-death experiences? Journal of Near-Death Studies. 2007, 25(4), 237–244.

Greyson, B, Broshek, DK, Derr, LL, and Fountain, NB. Mystical experiences associated with seizures. Religion, Brain & Behavior. 2015, 5(3), 182–196.

Griffiths, RR, Hurwitz, ES, Davis, AK, Johnson, MW, and Jesse, R. Survey of subjective "God encounter experiences": Comparisons among naturally occurring experiences and those occasioned by the classic psychedelics psilocybin, LSD, ayahuasca, or DMT. PLoS ONE. 2019, 14(4), e0214377–https://doi.org/10.1371/journal.pone.0214377. Editor: Rosemary Frey, University of Auckland.https://doi.org/10.1371/journal.pone.0214377.

Griffiths, RR, Richards, WA, McCann, U, and Jesse, R. Psilocybin can occasion mystical-type experiences having substantial and sustained personal meaning and spiritual significance. Psychopharmacology (Berl). 2006, 187(3), 268–283.

Griffiths, RR, Richards, W, Johnson, M, McCann, U, and Jesse, R. Mystical-type experiences occasioned by psilocybin mediate the attribution of personal meaning and spiritual significance 14 months later. Journal of Psychopharmacology. 2008, 22(6), 621–632.

Griffiths, RR, Johnson, MW, Richards, WA, Richards, BW, McCann, U, and Robert, J. Psilocybin occasioned mystical-type experiences: Immediate and persisting dose-related effects. Psychopharmacology. 2011, 218, 649–665.

Holden, J. Handbook of Near Death Experiences: Thirty Years of Investigation. Connecticut: Praeger Press, 2009.

Hood, RW, Hill, PC, and Spilka, BS. The Psychology of Religion: An Empirical Approach. New York: the Guilford Press, 2018.

Homer, The Iliad.

Huxley, A. The Perennial Philosophy. New York: Harper, 1944.

Huxley, A. The doors of perception and heaven and hell. New York: Harper Perennial Modern Classics, 1954.

James, W. The Varieties of Religious Experience. New York: Longmans, Green, And Co, 1917.

James, W. Does consciousness exist? Journal of Philosophy, Psychology and Scientific Methods. 1904, 1, 477–491.

James, W. Human Immortality: Two Supposed Objections to the Doctrine (2nd ed.). Boston & New York: Houghton, Mifflin, 1900/1898.

James, W. On pragmatism. In William James Writings 1902–1910. New York: Library of America. Literary Classics of the United States, Inc., 1987.

James, W. Principles of Psychology. New York: Cosimo Classics, 1890/2007, Vol I.

James, W. The Will to Believe and Other Essays in Popular Philosophy. New York: Dover Publications, Inc., 1897/1956.

Johnson, MW, Hendricks, PS, Barrett, FS, and Griffiths, RR. Classic Psychedelics: An integrative review of epidemiology, mystical experience, brain network function, and therapeutics. 2018, https://doi.org 10.1016/j.pharmthera. 2018.11.010

Johnson, MW, Garcia-Romeu, A, Cosimano, MP, and Griffiths, RR. Pilot study of the 5-HT2AR agonist psilocybin in the treatment of tobacco addiction. Journal of Psychopharmacology (Oxford, England). 2014, 28(11), 983–992.

Johnson, MW, Garcia-Romeu, A, and Griffiths, RR. Long-term follow-up of psilocybin-facilitated smoking cessation. The American Journal of Drug and Alcohol Abuse. 2017, 43(1), 55–60.

Jones, RM. Studies of Mystical Religion. London: Macmillan, 1909.
Joseph, R. The limbic system and the soul: Evolution and the neuroanatomy of religious experience. Zygon. 2001, 36, 105–136.
Καρανικόλας, ΠΚ. Γνόφος Αγνωσίας. Αθήναι: Αστηρ, 1980.
Katz, ST. Language, epistemology, and mysticism. Edited by ST Kantz. Mysticism and Philosophical analysis. New York: Oxford University Press, 1978.
Kelly, EF, Crabtree, A, and Marchal, P (Eds) Beyond Physicalism. Lanham: Rowman and Littlefield, 2015.
Kelly, EF, Kelly, EW, Crabtree, A, Gauld, A, Grosso, M, and Greyson, B. Irredussible Mind. Lanham: Rowman and Littlefield, 2007.
Koestler, A., The Invisible Writing. New York: The Macmillan Company, 1954.
Koestler, A. Return from Nirvana. London: Sunday Telegraph. March 12, 1961.
Leuba, JH. The Psychology of Religious Mysticism. New York: Harcourt, 1925.
Mackenna, S, and Page, BS (translators). Six Enneads by Plotinus. Global Grey e-books, 2014.
Maclean, KA, Leoutsakos, JM, Johnson, MW, and Griffiths, RR. Factor analysis of the mystical experience questionnaire: A study of experiences occasioned by the hallucinogen psilocybin. Journal for the Scientific Study of Religion. 2012, 51(4), 721–737.
Marshall, P. Mystical Encounters with the Natural World. New York: Oxford University Press, 2005.
Maslow, A. Religions, Values and Peak Experiences. Columbus OH: Ohio State University Press, 1964.
Moody, RA. Life after Life. Tracy, CA: Mokingbird Books, 1975.
Myers, FWH. Human Personality and Its Survival of Bodily Death. London: Longmans, Green, 1903, Vol. II.
New Testament: Revelations 10,6.
Nichols, DE. Psychedelics. Pharmacological Reviews. 2016, 68, 264–355.
Pahnke, WN. Drugs and Mysticism: An Analysis of the Relationship Between Psychedelic Drugs and the Mystical Consciousness. Cambridge, MA: Harvard University Press. 1963.
Pahnke, W. The psychedelic mystical experience in the human encounter with death. Psychedelic Review. 1971, 11, 1–15.
Papanicolaou, AC. et al. The Oxford Handbook of Functional Brain Imaging in Neuropsychology and Cognitive Neurosciences. New York: Oxford University Press, 2017.
Parnia, S. et al. AWARE—Awareness during resuscitation—A prospective study. Journal of Resuscitation. 2014, 85, 1799–1805.
Persinger, MA. The neuropsychiatry of paranormal experiences. Neuropsychiatric Practice and Opinion. 2001, 13, 515–524.
Persinger, MA. Modern neuroscience and near-death experiences: Expectancies and implications. Comments on "A neurobiological model for near-death experiences. Journal of Near-Death Studies. 1989, 7(4), 233–239.
Pfeiffer, F Meister Eckhart, translated by C de B. Evans London: J. M. Watkins, 1924, Vol.I.
Plato, Symposium
Plato, Philebus.
Plato, Phaedo.
Plato, Phaedrus.
Plutarch, Alcibiades. 19
Pindar, fragment 121 (Bowra).

Prabhavanandana, S, and Manchester, F. (translators) The Upanishads: Breath of the Eternal. Hollywood, California: The Vendanta Society of Southern California. Holywood, CA: New American Library (Mentor Books), 1957.

Richards, WA. Sacred Knowledge. New York: Columbia University Press, 2016.

Ring, K, and Valarino, EE. Lessons from the Light: What We Can Learn from the Near-Death Experience. New York: Insight Books, 2006.

Ring, K, Cooper, S, and Tart, C. Mindsight: Near-Death and Out-of-Body Experiences in the Blind. Palo Alto, CA: William James Center for Consciousness Studies at the Institute of Transpersonal Psychology), 1999.

Rolt, CE. (translator) Dionysius the Areopagite on the Divine Names and the Mystical Theology. New York: Macmillan, 1940/1957.

Ruck, CAP, Bigwood, J, Staples, D, and Wasson, GE. Journal of Psychedelic Drugs. 1979, 11 (1–2), 145–146.

Rucker, JH, Iliff, J, and Nutt, DJ. Psychiatry & the psychedelic drugs. Past, present & future. Neuropharmacology. 2018, 142, 200–218.

Sabom, M. Light and Death: One Doctor's Fascinating Account of Near Death Experiences. Grand Rapids MI: Zondervan, 1988.

Santayana, G. The Sense of Beauty. New York: Barns and Noble Publishing, Inc., 1896/2005.

Schultes, RE, Hofmann, A, and Ratsch, C. Plants of the Gods: Their Sacred, Healing, and Hallucinogenic Powers. Rochester, Vermont: Healing Arts Press, 2001.

Smith, H. Cleansing the Doors of Perception: The Religious Significance of Entheogenic Plants and Chemicals. Boulder CO: Sentient Publications, 2000.

Smith, M. Readings from the Mystics of Islam. London: Luzac & Company, Ltd., 1950.

Stace, WT. Mysticism and Philosophy. Los Angeles: Jeremy P. Tarcher, Inc., 1960.

Stace, WT. The Teachings of the Mystics. New York: Mentor Books, 1960.

Suzuki, DT. Zen Buddhism: Selected Writings of D.T, Suzuki. New York: Anchor Books, 1956.

Teresa, Saint. The Complete Works of Saint Teresa. Translated and edited by E. Allison Peers from the critical edition of P. Silverio de Santa Teresa, C. D. London: Sheed & Ward, Ltd., 1946; New York: Sheed & Ward, Inc., 1946, VoL I, Chapter 18.

Underhill, EM: A Study of the Nature and Development of Man's Spiritual Consciousness (1911). Twelfth edition published by E.P. Dutton in 1930. Republished by Dover Publications in Mineola, New York, 2002.

van Lommel, P, van Wees, R, Meyers, V, and Elfferich, I, and. Near-death experience in survivors of cardiac arrest: A prospective study in the Netherlands. The Lancet. 2001, 358(9298), 2039–2045.

van Ruysbroeck, J. The Adornment of the Spiritual Marriage, translated by C. A. Wynschenck Dom. London: Sons, Ltd., 1916; New York: E. P. Dutton & Co., Inc, 1916.

van Ruysbroeck, J. The Adornment of the Spiritual Marriage, translated by C. A. Wynschenck Dom. London: Sons, Ltd., 1916.

Wainwright, WJ. Mysticism: A study of its nature, Cognitive Value and Moral Implications. Sussex: The Harvester Press, 1981.

Wasson, RG, Hoffmann, A, and Ruck, CA. The Road to Eleusis (Thirtieth anniversary Edition). Berkeley: North Atlantic Books, 2008.

Wasson, RG. Soma: Divine Mushroom of Immortality. New York: Harcourt Brace Jovanovich, 1968/1971.

Zaehner, PC. Mysticism Sacred and Profane. New York: Oxford University Press, 1961.

Index